Jim & Judi,

In friendship,

Mike Hallee

You Are Rich
Discovering Faith in Everyday Moments

By
Michael Halleen

Wipf & Stock Publishers
Eugene, Oregon

YOU ARE RICH
Discovering Faith in Everyday Moments

Wipf and Stock Publishers
199 West 8th Avenue, Suite 3
Eugene, Oregon 97401

ISBN: 1-59752-343-7

Printed in the United States

for my wife, Barb

Contents

Preface

The best advice I ever received as a communicator came from Dr. Ernest T. Campbell, then minister of Riverside Church in New York City. He was leading a graduate seminar for preachers and told us to buy a small book with blank pages and to keep it with us at all times.

In this book we were to record stories that we heard or read and thoughts that occurred to us in the midst of the day—anything that might be used as what he called "color" in our preaching.

On regular occasions we were to read what we had written, always starting at the back of the book. The most recent material, Campbell reasoned, was most likely to be useful to us, and he suggested that we review that first.

I followed his counsel gladly, having found no effective way to keep track of the stories and word pictures that are a public speaker's gold. It was painful, however, to follow *all* Campbell's guidelines. He wanted us to throw the book away when it was full, maintaining that only material fresh to us is truly useful. That always hurt.

Then several years ago, my sister, Sue Awes, suggested that I start to tell some of the stories—items from my little books—that I had used in preaching over the years. She referred to a few of those that she remembered in particular and persuaded me that others would like to hear them too.

The result was a weekly e-mail column called *Monday Moments* which I have published since then. This book is a compilation of a number of those columns.

Each item is preceded by a brief passage from the Bible. My reflections are not an attempt to interpret or explain those passages in a systematic way. Instead, I have used them as stimuli for thoughts that I wanted to express—or stories I wanted to tell.

So far as I know, the stories that are not mine have come from sources that are in the public domain. A few came to my attention long ago and are no longer possible to trace. Some may have been subsequently published by others who found them in the same sources as I did, in publications unknown to me.

My thanks to Ernest Campbell for telling me to write the stories down. Thanks also to Sue for encouraging me to repeat them. And thanks to John Wipf—and many other of my *Monday Moments* readers—for urging me to put them out as a book.

Michael Halleen

Reflecting on Attitude

If you ever find happiness by hunting for it, you will find it as the old woman did her lost spectacles . . . safe on her own nose all the time.

—Josh Billings

Attitude

...To be made new in the attitude of your minds;
... (Ephesians 4:23)

Friday night was the biggest night of the week for us as high school football players. Tension built up all day, culminating in a meeting that started in the locker room two hours before game time. The head coach gave a brief speech, usually telling us all the things we had done wrong in practice that week, and then he sent us upstairs to the gym. There he had laid out mats on the floor, and we were to lie down and relax. "Get yourselves ready to play!" he would bark. "Think about what you will do! Get an attitude!"

It had not worked all that well in my senior year. We had won only about half our games, and now, close to the end of our schedule, we were getting ready to play our eternal enemies from Edina. We had not beaten them in a decade at least, but we lived in hope. I lay there full of nerves, trying to relax, hoping we would win, dreaming that I might have a role in it.

Then I heard the quiet voice of one of our assistant coaches in my ear. He said, "Mike, keep your eyes closed, and just listen. You have the best pair of hands I've ever seen on a high school pass receiver. You always seem to be able to get open, and I've never seen you drop a ball you should have caught. Tonight we're going to throw the ball a lot, and we want to throw it to you. Just do what you do so well, relax and have fun. You're the man."

He made no demands for change and had no complaints that I was a poor blocker and worse tackler. There were no threats that if I did not perform, I would be standing on the sidelines. This young coach simply affirmed the gifts I did have and praised the ability I did possess. My attitude swelled, filled my head, filled the whole room.

I wish I could say that we won the game that night, but no, it was another loss to big, bad Edina. But I played the game of my life—relaxed, calm, efficient, smooth. I caught passes I had no business catching and even made a few unexpected blocks and tackles. The head coach wondered, "What got into you tonight?" I told him about the voice in my ear and the new attitude in my heart. "Well, you looked like a new player," he growled.

I was. A new attitude about my skills, prospects, appearance, relationships, work—about myself—makes a new me.

Images

If anything is excellent or praiseworthy — think about such things. (Philippians 4:8)

I took a course in seminary that was built around one sentence: *You move toward that upon which you dwell.* We were assigned readings and experiments demonstrating the influence that expectations have on performance. The point was that we can improve the way we live by the way we view our lives and what we expect of them. Our mental images shape the way we live and provide the limits for our potential. What we think of ourselves, we become. What we expect to get from life, we get. I enjoyed the course and did well. Good images.

But I became a true believer when I went back to seminary for a graduate degree. The process took five years, and about halfway through I became very discouraged. The required dissertation seemed too big a task in the midst of my pastoral duties, and I began to doubt that it would ever be done.

I shared my feelings with a professor who had been helpful to me, and he gave me some advice that made all the difference. He said, "Every day spend a few minutes imagining yourself actually walking across the platform to get the degree. Visualize the steps. See President Hubbard smiling at you and shaking your hand. Feel the hood being placed on your shoulders. Imagine it! Expect it! Then nothing in the world can prevent it."

I did as he said. Each day I spent some moments dwelling on the end of all this effort and allowed myself to feel the gratification of succeeding. It was a positive focus, beyond the toil of paragraphs and pages that needed to be produced. I imagined myself being fulfilled on that stage, receiving that hood, shaking that hand. And when the day arrived and I walked across the platform, it was exactly as I had envisioned it. You move toward that upon which you dwell.

Expect to get sick in the spring and you certainly will. Expect to feel good today and you will see goodness rise up to bless you. Dwell on how often you have lost the sale and you are setting yourself up to fail again. Imagine finding warm receptions and positive responses and they are what you will receive.

The apostle knew this principle when he encouraged us to think about the things that are excellent and worthy of praise. Expect to be close to God! Imagine yourself enjoying life! Think of yourself contributing to a happy relationship! Dwell on faithfulness, hope, kindness (build your own list), and you will find yourself moving toward them.

Joy

Be joyful always. (1 Thessalonians 5:16)

Abraham Lincoln once said that people are just about as happy as they make up their minds to be. Happiness (or joyfulness)—understood not merely as giddy feelings but as an attitude of contentment—is, plain and simple, a matter of choice.

You can be unhappy if you want to be. It is easy to accomplish. Just tell yourself that things are not going well and that life is hard. Decide that circumstances are against you and that nothing is satisfying to you. I guarantee that you will be unhappy.

On the other hand, you can decide to be happy. You can say to yourself that things are looking good and that it is a pleasure to be alive. You can decide that the promises of the day await you and that you are ready for them. I promise that you will at least have a terrific chance of being happy.

We shall not be naive about life. Of course there are times of grief and days of trouble that cannot be overcome by simple words of good cheer. There are hard messages and sorrows of the heart that wear down even those most determined to seek joy. But the fact remains that, to a great extent, happiness—contentment—is a matter of choice.

Many of us religious types are all too ready to put responsibility for our feelings on God or the devil. We have fallen into a trap of seeing life's circumstances as being placed there by a cosmic force, part of our destiny. Worse, we allow those circumstances to control our feelings, as though we are helpless to do anything about them. It is God's will for me, we say. The devil is prowling around, causing me grief, we think. I will have to be unhappy until this passes, we suspect.

But when the apostle commended joyfulness to the early Christians, he did not suggest it was something that would *happen* to them. It was something to *do*. Happiness was not a state of being in some future time when things improved. It was an attitude to choose now, today. Happiness is our responsibility, not God's. Failure to find it is our doing, not the devil's.

Decide that you will be happy today. Believe that you can handle successfully whatever comes your way today. Say so out loud. Give thanks for your health and strength, whatever their level. Say so out loud. Consider how wonderful it is to be alive in the world God has made. Say so out loud. Remember the people in your life, whether many or few, and the mercy those relationships offer to you. Say it out loud. Repeat tomorrow, and the next day, and the next. Make it a habit.

It is your life. You can be just about as happy as you make up your mind to be.

Persist

Jesus told his disciples a parable to show them that they should always pray and not give up.
(Luke 18:1)

The parable Jesus told his friends in this instance was about a woman who had brought a matter before a judge in her town and then hounded and harassed him until he made a decision in her favor. She was relentless and simply would not accept any judgment except the one she had sought. "Pray that way," was the message Jesus had for his friends . . . and for us.

In one of his last public appearances Winston Churchill spoke at a university commencement. He stepped to the podium and said solemnly, "Never give up." He paused for a long time, then said again, "Never give up." Another long pause and, again, "Never give up!" Then he sat down. It was all he had to say.

Persistence, whether in prayer or in pursuit of our goals, is an enormous virtue. Vindication often comes simply through staying power, and victory often is given to the one who endures. After his defeat of Napoleon at Waterloo, Wellington said, "The British soldiers were not braver than the French; they were just braver five minutes longer."

Persistence needs to be measured, of course, against the goals which one is pursuing. To try week after week to win the lottery will likely be a waste of time and money. And persistence alone is not a guarantee of the exact results one may want. Some years ago the wire services carried a story of a Taiwanese man who wrote 700 love letters to his girl friend in the hopes she would marry him. She married the mailman who faithfully had delivered all those letters. There are no sure things in this life.

But persist anyway. Choose goals that matter. Be certain that they are worthy of you, and believe that you are worthy of reaching them. Do not listen to those who grumble, complain or quit. You cannot know how many steps may be needed to achieve your goals, only that when you stop taking them, you will find failure. The prize is given at the end of the journey, not at the beginning.

So take a step today, then another—one step at a time, one day at a time. Persist, and never give up.

Energy

Whatever you do, work at it with all your heart
.... *(Colossians 3:23)*

Betta Mengistu was a colleague of mine for several years, a man I came to admire for a number of his qualities, not the least of which was a driving energy.

An Ethiopian living and working in Nairobi, Kenya, Betta was a passionate and eloquent communicator. I once heard him speak at a large church in Detroit where he was required to preach at four services in five hours. I listened to each one and was amazed that instead of diminishing in energy and enthusiasm from one repetition to the next, he actually increased. As we finally went to lunch, I asked him why he was not tired after all that work. "Because," he said, "I believe absolutely in everything I said. I am enthusiastic about my convictions!"

Knute Rockne, the legendary football coach at Notre Dame, insisted that his players have their emotions under control and channeled in the right direction in order to maximize their energy levels. He refused to have a player on his team who did not have a genuinely friendly feeling for each of his fellow players. "I have to get the most energy out of a man," he said, "and that cannot happen if his energy is wasted on negative feelings toward others."

11

Energy is increased when we are on fire about something and maximized when it is focused on positive relationships and outcomes. We lose energy when life becomes dull, when our outlook is negative. Get interested in something. Throw yourself into it with abandon. Look beyond your own life and its familiar little circles. Do not sit around moaning about things, taking in negative news and wondering why someone is not doing something. If you are not involved in a cause bigger than yourself, you are probably tired and may feel like you are dying on the vine.

I watched my friend Wayne beaming from ear to ear at the end of an exhausting week working with 75 kids at an orphanage in Russia. The administration and staff there could not understand how we could keep going day after day and hour after hour. Wayne sat in the front seat of a new van—for which he had raised the money—that had just been delivered to the orphanage. There was no trace of tiredness, no hint of being weary—just a light in his eyes and a smile that had no bounds. "This is worthwhile," he said. "This is what matters."

If you lose yourself in something bigger than yourself—with conviction and positive feelings—you will find the energy you may be looking for.

Success

One thing I do: forgetting what is behind and straining forward to what is ahead, I press on toward the goal. (Philippians 3:13, 14)

Five of the world's greatest scientists came from Budapest, all of them within a generation. They included the father of the hydrogen bomb, one of the original splitters of the atom, a Nobel Prize winning physicist, a master mathematician, and the world's leading aeronautical scientist. They all had the same physics teacher in high school, a man who always considered himself a failure because he was just a teacher.

Success or failure cannot be measured in a moment. Both require time, without which our opinion is just a rush to judgment.

I officiated at the funeral of a woman who had lived with only her dog for a companion and who had died alone, without family nearby. I expected the service to be brief and poorly attended. The parlors of the funeral home were filled, however, as word of her death—and even of her whereabouts—had circulated throughout the region. She had moved from one town to another some years before, and people had lost touch. Now they came from everywhere and told of what her kindness had meant to them. Her own opinion had been that she was insignificant, a failure, and so she had let herself become lost when she had moved. But family and neighbors called her a shining light. They knew nothing of failure in her life.

The classic example of measuring success, of course, is the story of the man who entered the army as captain and returned a private, ending his military career. He opened a little shop in a country town, but the business failed. He started practicing law but was too impractical and temperamental to make a success of it. He lost an election for the state legislature. He failed in an attempt to be nominated for a seat in Congress and lost an election for a minor county job. He ran for Vice President of the United States and was defeated, then lost another race for a seat in the Senate. The only election he ever won—his last—was simply because the other candidates were bigger losers than he. His name: Abraham Lincoln.

Success and failure are only illusions until the test of time has been passed.

A college administrator told me of expelling a bright young student who had repeatedly skipped classes and failed exams, had no sense of purpose and was consistently in trouble—a hopeless case. "And he is now the president of the University of Washington," my friend said.

I will reserve judgment about success and failure, including my own. I will take another step today and keep moving. Time alone reveals the meaning—and the measure—of success.

Paradigm

We consider blessed those who have persevered.
You have heard of Job's perseverance and have seen
what the Lord finally brought about. (James 5:11)

A crossword puzzle clue "Paradigm of patience" seemed to have only one logical answer: Job ("the patience of Job"). Unfortunately, this one had to be four letters long so I had to look elsewhere, but it got me to thinking about Job, and I assigned myself the topic of perseverance—patience that goes beyond mere waiting—as the lesson I would teach in an upcoming mission to a Russian orphanage.

What I told those kids was that there are only two roads that lead to an important goal: strength and perseverance. Strength is a quality that only a few are privileged to have, but perseverance can be employed by the smallest and weakest of us. It rarely fails in its purpose because its silent power grows irresistibly greater with time.

I told them that very few successful people started out successful. Theodore Geisel (Dr. Seuss) took his first book to 20 publishers before the 21st accepted it. Thomas Edison had thousands of failures before his electric light bulb worked. The Wright brothers crashed a hundred times before the first airplane flew.

Hope is a fragile thing. The ease with which we become discouraged in any effort can move us quickly to a point of inertia, and we give up. We assume that the obstacles will defeat us and that ultimately we will fail. We are not, we tell ourselves, among the strong.

The key is in keeping on, another step and then another, pushing ahead despite our feelings—no surrender. The 16th century Spanish explorer Hernan Cortes, after landing in Mexico, ordered his crew to burn their ships so there would be no retreat. He thus committed himself and his people not only to survival in this new world but to conquering whatever obstacles came their way. Extreme, perhaps, in an alien land, but there is something compelling about kicking the props out from underneath and committing absolutely to persist in the path one has chosen.

A Chinese proverb says "Great souls have wills; feeble ones have only wishes." Great souls achieve great things in life, not so much by strength as by perseverance. Thus Job became our paradigm of patience.

I will never know what may be brought about in the lives of the orphaned kids, but I am sure that they—as we—will find blessing only as they find the will to persevere.

Worry

Do not worry about tomorrow, for tomorrow will worry about itself. Each day has enough trouble of its own. (Matthew 6:34)

Worry is a worrisome thing. I can hear and believe all kinds of good advice about it, but it still shows up at my door. Friends tell me not to worry about things I have said or done—about mistakes I have made—and I want to think they are right, but I worry that they are not, so I worry anyway. Even when Jesus tells me not to worry, still it is there. To shake off worrying is hard.

The thing that has helped me more than anything else is to try to see each day in relationship to the larger goals of a lifetime. Someone once told me to "play the averages." A baseball player who gets a hit every third time at bat is headed for the Hall of Fame. A salesperson who receives a one percent return on a blind mailing will do very well in that year. Authors ultimately are remembered for their best work, not for trials and errors along the way. It is the long run that matters, and each day, each effort, contributes something to the larger goals that shape the meaning of my life.

Ralph Waldo Emerson told of a friend who, whenever he

planned his budget for a journey, included a certain percentage to lose to robbers. That way, he reasoned, his trip would not be spoiled if he lost some money. It had been budgeted.

President John F. Kennedy read several newspapers every morning and often became agitated about things that were said about him. When his aides would arrive to help plan his day, Kennedy would say, "However, . . ." With that one word he swept away frustration and anger and got on with what needed to be done. Criticism was part of a president's budget for the day. Jesus said we would do well to budget some trouble daily. That way, when we meet it—as we surely will—it will not spoil the day and deter our progress toward those lifetime goals.

We know from accounts of others on board that Columbus' journey to the new world was not an easy one. The crew was often disgruntled and afraid because of the uncertainty of their fate. At one point there was even an attempted mutiny. Yet Columbus' log for that day read: "We sailed forward today, course west by southwest." Was he worried? Probably. Did he take his worries seriously? Certainly. But focus on the larger goal kept daily worries in perspective.

There may be some trouble today. Budget for it. Plan to sail forward.

Morning

(God's) mercies never fail; they are new every morning. (Lamentations 3:22, 23)

Mrs. Miller, our fifth grade teacher at Brookside School, was a stickler for a neat classroom. One day she advised us that pencils left on our desks at the end of the day would be collected and not returned. And when it happened, when the grinch actually took the pencils of several classmates, it seemed time for action. My friend Johnny and I wrote and circulated a petition declaring Mrs. Miller "entirely too mean" and calling on the principal to "require her to stop this unfair practice." Not bad for fifth grade revolutionaries.

We gathered signatures on the playground at noon, only to find our teacher waiting for us at the door of our room when we returned. She was crying. One of the girls in the class, Ruth Ann, had told on us. (Thus in my mind that name has forever been linked with treachery: *Brutus, Benedict, Ruth Ann.*)

We reported to the principal's office, waiting an hour or so for our mothers to arrive and the axe to fall. But it never fell. I am sure the long-forgotten lecture was appropriate for the occasion, but all I remember—other than the stern look of my mother—is the last sentence of Mrs. Swellin, the principal: "Now, boys, you may return to your class, and you can begin again."

You can begin again. Yesterday was not great, but today is new. I can begin again. Our words got us in trouble last night, but today we will be more careful how we speak to one another. We can begin again. I let things go last week that I really wanted to do, but this is a new week. I can begin again. Some of our decisions in the past have been less than wise, but this is a new opportunity. We can begin again.

It is true, of course, that some of those harsh words or failed opportunities or bad decisions in the past may make the present more difficult. But I do not need to repeat them. God's mercies are new every morning. Every moment offers a new chance to grow, to go forward, to love. Today I can forgive. Today I can let go of the guilt of a past mistake. Today I can fulfill a promise.

Today I can begin again.

Age

Do not cast me away when I am old; do not
forsake me when my strength is gone. (Psalm 71:9)

Agatha Christie, the mystery writer, was married to a distinguished British archaeologist, M.E.L. Mallowan. She was once asked if it was difficult being married to a man who was away from home so often in his study of ancient cultures and exploration of old ruins. She responded that it was actually an advantage being married to an archaeologist "because the older I get, the more interested he becomes in me."

We treat our aging with humor because we have not figured out other ways to deal with it that do not lead to despair. Yet aging is nothing more than a natural progression from one stage of life to the next. Each stage has its problems, and none of them is the perfect one. Where we are right now is just the right phase for us at this point in life. To accept it with grace promotes enthusiasm, wisdom and beauty within our souls every day. It enables us to be more honest and free.

It has been said that at age 20 we worry about what others think of us, at 40 we don't care what they think of us, and at 60 we discover they haven't been thinking of us at all. Having made the last of those discoveries, I am trying to accept my age. It is where I am, and there is nothing to do but live it to the fullest.

The days of our lives are precious things that cannot be stored up, held in keeping for some future time. We have to use them, and the blessing is that the more we do, the more of life we find we really have. I remember my aged grandfather reading for hours even when he had to use a large magnifying glass just to see the words. His occasional grumblings of approval or disapproval showed that he was engaged in something that mattered to him. Pablo Casals, the foremost cellist of the 20th century, was asked when he was more than 90 years old why he practiced five or six hours a day, and he said it was because he was "still improving."

President Franklin Delano Roosevelt asked Oliver Wendell Holmes, Jr., the great Supreme Court justice, why he was reading Plato. "To improve my mind, Mr. President," he answered. Holmes was 92.

Most important, in whatever phase of aging we are passing through, we can see ourselves as persons who matter, who have a part in God's plans. We want to avoid the snare of thinking of ourselves as "just" something—*just* a housewife, *just* a kid, *just* an old man. The Psalmist saw himself as "God's somebody." Though frail and imperfect, he considered himself worthy of being remembered, of being counted, of serving.

We can do the same.

Vocation

I took you from the ends of the earth, from its farthest corners I called you. (Isaiah 41:9)

A woman supporter of the Confederacy during the Civil War was said to have freed dozens of southern prisoners of war by simply visiting Union Army camps and asking to see her son. The camps were too crowded and disorganized for anyone to pay attention to another mother seeking her child, so she would be told to find him on her own. She would walk among the prisoners until she found a Confederate officer and offer him the civilian clothes she had packed in the bottom of her food basket. The two of them would then leave the camp by another way, just another couple come to inquire about family.

Finally captured, she went on trial for espionage. She pleaded not guilty, saying she was not a spy. "I am a Liberator!" she said. "I set men free!" She had a nobler view of her vocation.

"Vocation" means "calling," the bidding of a Higher Power that has brought us to where we are and which moves us toward where we want—or ought—to be. The Bible makes it clear that we have been called not merely to an occupation or profession. Our true vocation is to discipleship and caring for others.

The Liberator would have appreciated the story of two boys

23

who lived in a town where the chief industry was an airline manufacturing plant. They were asked what their fathers did for a living, and the first replied that his dad was a riveter. The second, whose father was also a riveter, said proudly, "My dad builds airplanes."

The difference is profound. Words reflect what we think of ourselves, the sense we have not just of what we do but of who we are. So I did my best work for the ministry I represented in Russia when I borrowed back a title I had once held in that organization, that of Regional Vice President. It opened doors for me that would otherwise have been closed because people there respected a vice president the way we do those who build airplanes. Anything less was just a "riveter." Perhaps more important, it also opened doors in me to a better sense of my own worth and ability.

Robert Louis Stevenson said, "To be what we are, and to become what we are capable of becoming, is the only end of life." The calling which we have received—and the way in which we name that calling—make a difference in how we think of ourselves and therefore how we live. The words we use about ourselves and the descriptions we accept as applying to us orient us to those ends for which we have been created. They describe our sense of worth in our own eyes . . . as well as in the eyes of God.

Worthy

*For he will command his angels concerning you
to guard you in all your ways. (Psalm 91:11)*

My only memory of kindergarten is of a woven rag rug that
my parents were required to supply for me to use for a daily rest
period. What I actually remember is being sentenced to sit on
that rug for several minutes—the equivalent, I suppose, of the
more contemporary "time-out." The teacher was supposed to
tap me on the head when my time of silent discipline had ended,
but she apparently forgot about me and left me there for the
afternoon. I sat and stared at the rug, my head bowed, thinking
my time of penance might never end. I must be, I thought, a
very bad boy.

Years later as a seminary student I stood at a grocery counter
in California unable to sign a check. The cashier stood waiting,
but my hand would not move to start the first letter of my name.
I tried to look casual, but in fact I simply could not get the muscles
to operate. "Whoops," I said, "I just realized I have the wrong
checkbook with me," and hurried out of the store, leaving the
groceries on the counter. It was a lie. We had only one checkbook and were barely able to keep *that* account alive. But I had
to save face somehow, and there would have been no way to

explain—in fact I did not even know—what was happening.

The following week I shared my grocery store humiliation with a professor. He asked me to tell him a story from my childhood, and I told him about that afternoon on the rug. He said, "It was that little boy who couldn't sign the check the other day. You must have felt awful. Has anyone ever told you that you're a wonderful person? Do you know how much you're loved?" I told him my wife said things like that. "But," he asked, "do you believe her? Do you ever say things like that about yourself?" I had to allow that I did not talk like that about myself at all. "Try it," he said as he dismissed me from his office. "There's a child in there who needs to hear it." I did and have never since had a problem signing my name.

We are what we are today because of what we were—and what we thought we were—at five and fifteen and thirty-five. Memories of hurts from our past live on long after their time. The answer is love for ourselves, accepting our value in the world. Those who tell us of that love, who express our worthiness even when we feel none, are angels of God sent to guard us in our way.

You count . . . You matter . . . You are worthy . . . You are wonderful. And when the voice speaking such love is our own, it is no less angelic and, perhaps, all the more powerful.

Considering Direction

Ideals are like stars: you will not succeed in touching them with your hands, but like the seafarer on the desert of waters, you choose them as your guides, and, following them, you reach your destiny.

—Carl Schurz

Home

Like a bird that strays from its nest is a man
who strays from his home. (Proverbs 27:8)

G.K. Chesterton was among the great thinkers and original writers of the 20th century. He was also among the most absent-minded. He had difficulty keeping dates straight and often showed up a day early for a lecture or a week late for an appointment. And he was frequently lost in the busy streets of London. On one famous occasion he sent a telegram to his wife: *Am in Market Harborough. Where ought I to be?*

Under the willow tree at the edge of the lake that fronts our house there is a small protected area along the shore in which floating objects collect throughout the summer. They never intend to end up there, imagining, I am sure, that they will be floating free forever. But they get stuck for a time—leaves, small branches, a duck feather, the occasional shoe or abandoned life-preserver. The motion of the waves and the summer breeze do not seem to touch anything in that little backwater, and it becomes a holding pond for lost objects. *Where ought I to be?*

There are times when we find ourselves in such places in life, stuck in some inlet, out of the flow, away from the action, untouched by the wind. It feels as though our plans have been put on hold. It seems at times that we shall have to spend the winter, perhaps even a lifetime, in this backwater collection point. What can we do to break out again into open water? *Where ought I to be?*

When Chesterton's wife received his telegram, she sent a one-word message in return: *Home.* She explained later that it was easier to get him home and start him off in the right direction than to try to tell him how to get from where he was to where he was supposed to be. *Home.*

My golf coach used to say that the most important element in the golf swing is the grip. It is the only point of contact between the player and the club used to accomplish the player's goal. The coach would pace up and down behind us on the practice range saying, "Get a fresh grip now; get a fresh grip."

When you are stuck, get back to basics. Review the plan. Remember your purpose. Return to the point of contact with the Higher Power. Get a fresh grip. Go home. You can find a new start—in the right direction—from there.

Listening

He who has an ear, let him hear what the Spirit says . . . . (Revelation 3:22)

Years ago I read a story of a celebration planned to honor the driver of the one millionth car to cross a certain bridge. A large crowd had gathered, a band was playing, local dignitaries were all present, and the leader of the festivities was counting off the last dozen cars as they crossed the bridge.

A little red car came along, and it was apparent that this would be the millionth one. But the driver had his car windows up and, with his radio blaring, was oblivious to the whole thing. He saw the crowd and the blocked road and thought there must have been an accident. So he made a quick U-turn and started driving away. The crowd waved and shouted and somehow got him to stop so he could receive all the gifts and attention waiting for him.

Amazed at becoming such a celebrity, the driver confessed, "I almost missed it because I was listening to something else."

We sometimes miss the things that matter because we are focused on something else, tuned in only to familiar sounds and favorite voices. The mercy is that people occasionally come into our lives at the right time and get our attention. Like the crowd shouting to the driver, they wake us up and startle us into a new focus.

Ever since I had been a young boy people had said to me, "I suppose you're going to be a preacher, just like your grandpas." I denied it every time. Road block, U-turn. Three different majors in college, the last being education. Then there came that Saturday morning in Jon and Mary Ellen Braun's kitchen when Jon said to me, "If you want to teach, why don't you teach what you know is the most important thing in the world?" I turned my music down at that moment, wound down the window and heard my name being called. I had almost missed it because I had not been listening.

It has been my experience to hear the Spirit speak through people who care enough to keep me from driving away when I ought to be paying attention. God communicates through family, friends, colleagues, even strangers.

Of course, not every suggestion is life-changing, or even helpful. Not every opinion is worth considering. Sometimes it is good to keep the windows rolled up. But occasionally the commotion on the bridge is meant for me.

As time has gone on, I have become more and more aware that when I miss the Spirit's call, it is not for lack of a voice but for lack of listening. It is because the windows are up and the familiar noises of life are all that I hear.

Credentials

By what authority are you doing these things? . . .
And who gave you this authority? (Matthew 21:23)

Years ago a young woman who had been adopted as an infant asked me to help her make contact with her birth mother. She had found her mother after an extensive search but was afraid to call because she was not sure what kind of response she would receive.

The daughter's fears were well founded: the mother was frightened by the prospect of contact. Her husband, who was not the father, had never known of this pre-marital birth, and she was fearful of his reaction. To try to allay the mother's fears, I made some unwarranted promises as a pastor about the proposed contact. They were not at all what the daughter intended, and she confronted me in anger. "What right did you have?" she demanded to know. "Who said you could make promises for me?"

She was absolutely right, of course. In my enthusiasm for a reunion I had said too much and made commitments that were not my right to offer. I had no authority to speak as I did, especially so because I had no substantial relationship with either person.

In Meredith Willson's wonderful play *The Music Man*, members of the school board in River City are continually trying to get Professor Harold Hill to show them his credentials. By whose authority is he selling the townspeople all these musical instruments and claiming to be able to lead a marching band?

The wily professor, who has no credentials at all, keeps putting off these officials while at the same time moving throughout the town winning friends and helping people feel good about themselves, so that in the end credentials are no longer an issue. His authority has been established by the relationships he has built. He has earned the right by simply winning people to himself.

I thought of Professor Hill when I, as a representative of a Bible translation and publishing ministry, was seated at lunch next to the mayor of the town of Galich, Russia and she asked me by whose authority we were translating the Bible again into Russian. I had no papers that would have satisfied her bureaucratic curiosity, so I decided to try to strike up a friendship. By the end of our day's visit, she was thanking me for our efforts and wished us well.

Positions and titles are not our best claim to authority or rights. The integrity we establish by building relationships is the most significant—and powerful—credential we possess.

Indecision

Therefore I tell you, do not worry about your life, what you will eat or drink, or about your body, what you will wear. Is not life more important than food, and the body more important than clothes? (Matthew 6:25)

Joseph Henry, founder of the Smithsonian Institutions, grew up in the early 19ᵗʰ century, a time when one's shoes were made to order by the local cobbler. Henry went to have his feet measured for a pair of shoes his grandmother was buying for him and could not decide between the two styles the shoemaker offered, round-toed or square-toed. Henry said he made half a dozen trips to the cobbler's shop over the next few days but still was unable to make a decision.

On his last visit he found the shoes ready—one had a round toe and the other a square toe. Joseph Henry said, "I had to wear those monuments to indecision for a long time, and they taught me, as nothing else could, the penalty one must pay for indecisiveness."

My own lesson on indecision came shortly after I received my driver's license as a teenager. I remember driving past her house in my '49 Ford convertible (well used but dearly loved), then around and around the block, wondering if I dared knock on her door. After many uncertain circuits, I found a '53 Chevy parked in her driveway, and its driver was standing at the front door talking to her, inviting her for a ride. They waved as I drove by . . . the penalty I had to pay for indecisiveness.

Life is full of choices. Every day we come to places where the road divides (paint the house white or ivory?), sometimes in a hundred directions (or cream?). Some of those choices really matter, but probably fewer of them (eggs or pancakes?) than we think at the time. Some are tougher than others, but most are not as tough (brown shoes or black?) as we make them out to be. Some bring results that we must live with for a while (remodel or buy new?), but we are probably more able to adjust to those consequences than we suspect.

The fact is life is made up of the thousand little decisions I will make today, and the time I spend worrying about them, at the moment or in retrospect, is time lost in the more important matter of living through them and with them, finding benefit and growth along whatever road I have chosen. Look . . . consider . . . decide . . . and then go. Do not look back. Your life awaits you.

Sails

Let us not love with words or tongue but with actions and in truth. (1 John 3:18)

Statistics show that more than six billion greeting cards are sent out every year in the U.S., the equivalent of about 20 per person. (Someone must be taking on extra responsibility for my shortfall.) Hallmark thrives because we realize that we cannot ask someone we love simply to assume our love. It needs to be expressed, even if the words are those of a professional writer in Kansas City, unrelated to the sender and unknown to the beloved. Every sensible person involved in a relationship of love knows the importance of expressing that love.

Every sensible person knows also that the words alone are not enough. Love is better seen than described. To speak of love and not to show it reveals a love is at the least shallow, at the worst untrue. Oscar Hammerstein wrote, "A bell is not a bell until you ring it, and love is not love until you give it."

When Pele, the greatest soccer player of all time, played his last match in October 1977, he had 76,000 people in the stands chanting "Love! Love! Love!" throughout the game. Somehow he was able to dramatize with his feet and smile and athletic ability what he could never have adequately verbalized: people's desire to care about something together across all divisions of nation, race and hemisphere.

An acquaintance told me of her new teaching job at a private school in the East. The school had gone through five headmasters in six years and now had taken on another, a man with a military background who had promised to bring order. Instead he brought *orders*—issuing memos and directives in abundance. Throughout the fall term the school was in an uproar, worse than it had ever been. Most conversations were in anger or in criticism.

In January, the teacher wrote a single sentence on the board: "Let there be love in this place, and let it begin with me." The next day she brought a planter and placed it on the headmaster's desk with no name attached. After that came candy, then cards, then notes of support to staff. Somehow, in a matter of weeks, there came to be a difference at the school. Relaxation, patience and cordiality replaced memos, discipline and tension. One person's love had turned around an institution.

A curious boy exploring a New England fishing wharf asked a fisherman, an old salt of the sea, what made the wind blow. The sailor replied, "Don't know, son. I can't say. But I know how to hoist a sail."

Who can explain how love works? Who needs to? Hoist a sail.

Improvising

Take no bag for the journey, or extra tunic, or sandals or a staff . . . (and) when they arrest you, do not worry about what to say or how to say it. (Matthew 10:10, 19)

In my first year out of seminary I was invited to speak at a series of meetings in a country church in southern Minnesota. It began on Ash Wednesday with a service of repentance. That had never been part of the calendar in my home church, so I had no idea what to expect. Apparently my host pastor did not either, because as we walked across the yard of his home to the church next door, he stopped and said, "We don't have any ashes!"

He ran back to the house and returned with a newspaper, some matches and a cereal bowl. We dug a small pit in the snow, stuffed the paper into it and lit a fire. The ashes blackened the melted snow to make a kind of soggy soot which, as we stirred it in the bowl, turned out to be a usable—if unpleasant look-ing—substance to be part of our liturgy.

With a sense of triumph and relief, we walked into the church with our bowl full of treasure. One by one, the people came for-ward and received a slightly soggy, sooty fingerprint on their brow. It was the start of a time of renewal in that little congregation.

Improvised grace.

When Jesus sent his friends out to do their work in his behalf, it was with no extra baggage and no prepared speeches. Most of what lay ahead of them would have to be improvised. One cannot plan every moment or be ready for every contingency.

There you are, in the emergency room or in the kitchen, at your desk or at the wheel. All around you is confusion, pain, need—and someone is looking to you as a source for contact with hope, sanity, relief—even contact with God. There is no opportunity to look up that Bible passage someone quoted or dig up that inspirational tape you once heard. It is just you and your willingness to improvise on the faith you have, or wish you had. And from somewhere deep inside there comes a promise: "Do not be afraid. I am with you."

We cannot always wait for grace to come to us. Sometimes we have to improvise it without knowing just what the right thing is to do. We have to try something and see what might come of it.

So take the chance. Fill out that application . . . Contact that adoption agency . . . Take that trip . . . Send that check . . . Make that phone call. Create some ashes in the snow, and expect good things to happen. Do not be afraid. Improvise grace.

Destiny

Let love and faithfulness never leave you; bind them around your neck, write them on the tablet of your heart. (Proverbs 3:3)

Roger Kahn wrote a fascinating book about the old Brooklyn Dodgers baseball team of the 1950s called *The Boys of Summer*. He had crisscrossed America to see what kind of harvest had followed its members after their World Series championship summer of 1955.

Twenty years later Kahn found one former Dodger was a recovering alcoholic, another was running a tiny grocery store in the Ozarks, and still another had been crippled for life in an auto accident. One had been voted into the Hall of Fame despite enduring personal difficulties. Some had faded into obscurity, others were merely aging with dignity. Kahn observed that all had found the destinies they had earned through choices they had made along the way.

The book reminded me of a question my young daughter asked long ago. She was standing in the back seat of the car and leaning over my shoulder (it was in the days before seat belts and car seats) and said, "Daddy, when we get where we're going, where will we be?" That is a mouthful for a kid and a good question for anyone to ponder.

Human beings are the only segment of creation that can determine its destiny. By changing our thoughts, we can change our lives. It is more than making resolutions. It is a matter of imagining where we would like to be, of creating a picture of what we would like our lives to look like a year from now. By dwelling on the goal, by creating a mental picture of ourselves enjoying the success that goal represents, we can actually begin to move in the direction of achieving it.

Some, of course, waste this precious ability by dreaming of wealth and luxury. How much better it would be to set a goal of becoming a good listener. How much more valuable it would be to imagine deepening my relationships, loving my children, understanding my colleagues, being faithful to my friends. In any case, we decide for ourselves the direction in which we would like to move.

Positive change seldom occurs accidentally or to those who are surprised by it. Destiny is a matter of choice, not chance. Those who set goals—and who write them on their hearts—are the ones who see changes happen. And the choices we make today become the rewards we find bound around our necks when we arrive at where we are going.

Just Do It

Do not be afraid; keep on speaking, do not be silent. (Acts 18:9)

Most of us, it seems, are eager to start new initiatives and set new goals, but few seem able consistently to carry them to conclusion. We get bogged down and, looking for a fresh start, we try something else, abandoning the old scheme long before its time. And we do it without analyzing our progress or celebrating our successes—often even without comment. We are good at starting races but have little commitment to finishing them. The beginning of a race is full of anticipation and high hopes, but the rewards are at the finish line.

One factor in reaching personal or group success is my willingness to do what is in front of me. I need to realize the value of what I am doing today in achieving a goal. Yes, others may be more qualified or able. No, I am not the only one on whom success depends. But I am here, and the need is here, so let us get on with it. If I were to have the privilege of writing a modern beatitude, it might be something like "Blessed are those who fulfill the positions they occupy."

At a summer camp for orphaned kids in Russia, I was part of a team providing the craft program. Fifty teenagers jammed into the room, ready for the activity for the day. They were to make a complicated (to me) bracelet of beads, using a weaving pattern that I had never really understood in our minimal training. I looked around for the team member scheduled to lead the session and saw her outside, bidding an extended farewell to some other kids who had to return to their orphanage early. There was nothing to do but take over. I focused on our commitment to a primary goal—that the kids were there for enjoyment. Perfect craft projects were not the object. The kids caught on quickly, even with my faulty leadership, and success was achieved.

Speak and do not be silent, the apostle was told. Do not be afraid to take on the job that is hard for you. You may not be the perfect person for it, but there you are. The opportunity and privilege have fallen to you. Right now no one else can do it better.

Those around you will benefit from your commitment, and—here is the wonderful thing—you may ultimately find yourself being carried a step closer to that which you were born to do, are compelled to do by the nature of the spirit that dwells within you.

Find the joy that awaits a good finish.

Timing

Whoever watches the wind will not plant;
whoever looks at the clouds will not reap.
(*Ecclesiastes 11:4*)

There is never seems to be a good time to do anything. The weather is never just right for planting or a picnic or a parade— or for anything else, it seems. It is never a good time to raise money, never the right time to schedule a retreat. It is never a good time to go back to school, never the right time to raise a family. It is never a good time to start a business, never the right time to fall in love. But if we wait for just the right time, not much happens.

Leaders are those who are willing to forge ahead even when the wind blows against them. Success is not found in waiting for the perfect moment. I was part of a group of clergy who went to the president of our denomination some years ago and urged him strongly to delay implementing a plan to raise funds for growth. Our case was logical and sensible, backed by all the right reasons: the time was not right, the organizational work had not been completed, and people were worried. The clouds were hanging too heavy right now. He heard us patiently and de- cided—as he must have known all along he would do—to go ahead with the campaign.

The effort succeeded beyond all forecasts. It took a leader who was willing to go beyond waiting for the perfect time to make it happen. Determination and perseverance were more to the point than cautious reading of the winds.

Unfortunately, many of us are merely wind-watchers and cloud-testers. We want to know what may be next, and we are glad to hear the counsel of anyone who will give us their interpretation of the seasons. We take polls and canvass the great and the ordinary as to how they read the signs of the times. We live defensively and passively, waiting for a signal that never comes. We have become a generation of onlookers rather than the daring pioneers our forebears were.

The late comedian, Flip Wilson, had a routine in which he was asked about his religion, and he said he was a "Jehovah's Bystander. They wanted me to be a Witness," he said, "but I didn't want to get involved."

If you want to be involved, do it now. That manuscript you are planning to submit . . . that restaurant you want to open . . . that relationship you are willing to try to mend . . . why not now? There will never be a perfect time, so why not use this imperfect one?

Hope

I do believe; help me overcome my unbelief!
(Mark 9:24)

A new neighbor bought the house two doors from ours at a ridiculously inflated price and set about remodeling. For six months he and his contractor tried one alternative after another, but they were unable to come up with anything the owner liked.

One day we discovered that the place had been leveled. The only solution had been to take it down to the ground and start over. What went up in its place was a castle in the midst of a neighborhood of modest ramblers. Sometimes the new house—or the new neighbor—is not what we had hoped for.

And in fact, many of our efforts go badly. The end of the war does not bring peace. The model airplane does not fly. The new job is dull. The romantic weekend is marred by sickness. The trip to Florida is ruined by bad weather. The family reunion falls short of expectations. The evening class you offer on world issues is canceled for low enrollment. The new car is a lemon. Many—maybe most—of our efforts go badly. But we want to believe. We want to have hope.

It is a mercy of life that small things happen to restore hope to our souls.

- A good night's sleep gives you a new lease on life.
- Time heals a wound of separation.
- The sickness goes away and strength is renewed.
- The colors of spring replace the drabness of March.
- The crystal goblet you drop in the sink bounces but does not break.
- The checks you wrote last week are about to bounce but do not because you forgot about an obscure bank holiday that makes your deposit on time after all.
- The last of the leaves get raked because there was enough bounce in your step to get you off the couch.

You are feeling good, feeling hopeful. Small miracles, big mercies.

Ken Medema is a musician known for composing songs on the spot to fit the substance and mood of the meeting he is attending. Often his words and their musical context provide an entire conference with an expression of its very soul. Years ago, he concluded the final session of a conference with this song:

> *There's a place as clean as a mountain stream*
> *And as bright as an April morn;*
> *There's a place for rebuilding a shattered dream,*
> *There's a place where hope is reborn.*
> *There's a place that is open to all this day,*
> *It's a place for all women and men;*
> *It's a place that is only a step away,*
> *It's a place of beginning again.*

My new neighbor is beginning again. He still has hope. I wish him well.

Shortcuts

*God led the people around by the desert road
toward the Red Sea. (Exodus 13:18)*

The Hastings cutoff is a back road that takes three miles off
the trip between Hastings and Red Wing in southern Minnesota. I love shortcuts, and when I learned of this one many years
ago, I felt the same sort of satisfaction one feels at finding a suit
for half price or picking up an antique at a steal. But then I told
a friend about it, and because he did not know the road and was
driving too fast one night, he missed a sharp curve and went
racing down a mud path intended only for cows. It took two
hours to get his car out of the field.

Apparently there were to be no shortcuts to the Promised
Land. The long way was the only way home for the Hebrew
people fleeing Egypt. Some cutoffs were known to them, like
the road through the land of the Philistines, but the people were
not ready to handle the obstacles they would meet there.

John Bunyan, in *Pilgrim's Progress*, tells of Bypath Meadow
which seemed to the Pilgrims, Christian and Hopeful, to be an
easier path than the Narrow Way, but they soon fell into the hands
of Giant Despair. The long way is God's way, the best way.

The long way around was a hard way for the Hebrew people.

Life was a struggle in that wilderness. But they learned discipline. They overcame the slave mentality they had had in their former life. They came to understand the principles by which life was to be lived. They developed leaders, made commitments, found wisdom. Shortcuts are no good for achieving results like that.

Some of us face roundabout roads on our journeys to our promised lands. It is important to remember that God's thoughts are long, long thoughts. God thinks not in moments or days, but in ages and eons, caring more about our journey than about our destination. God's purpose is not merely to see us arrive but to make something of us along the way. It is the building of grace in us that counts, the development of character that matters. Humans make the straight canal; God makes the winding river.

These days when I drive to Red Wing, I take old Highway 61, the long way around. It reminds me that there are no shortcuts to the things that really matter in life.

Come

Do your best to get here before winter. (2 Timothy 4:21)

Sitting in a Roman dungeon and feeling the winds of autumn blowing through his barren cell, the apostle Paul wrote to his trusted young disciple, Timothy, and asked him to visit. He wanted Timothy to bring him some books to read and paper to write on—and, oh yes, his coat—the old one he had left in the home of a friend, not having imagined he would spend the winter in jail. Come soon, Paul urged him. "Do your best to get here before winter."

There are matters in the lives of some of us that cannot wait until spring. Voices in our hearts are whispering to us to do our best to get here before winter, and we know that if we do not respond, what they ask of us now will not be done at all. If they are not answered soon, it is likely they never will be. The snows of winter are coming, and it is possible they will cover the grave of some great opportunity—or of some great friend.

"Come before winter." Timing matters. When I lived in Detroit we visited the Ford Motor Company's River Rouge facility. In the steel mill there I saw enormous glowing ingots taken from the furnace and rolled the length of the mill, being flattened and lengthened—changed at just the right moment. To one side lay the rejects that had cooled too fast. They had buckled and twisted and hardened to the point where change was no longer possible.

An engaged couple sat in my office and explained why they were delaying plans for their wedding. They wanted to take time to get to know one another better. A few months later they said they wanted to save some more money, and they were still getting to know each other. Six months later there was further delay because they were pursuing new goals that job changes had made necessary—and they were still getting to know one another. It was clear that all they had to look forward to was a very long engagement. I told them about the steel mill.

"Before winter" suggests that there is such a thing as "too late." We need to make changes when we can. An old rabbi used to say, "Repent the day before you die!" His people protested that they did not know the day of their death, so they did not know when to repent. "Then repent today!" the rabbi demanded.

Winter is coming. What is done today is done in time.

Thinking About Faith

The steps of faith fall on the seeming void,
But find the rock beneath.
                            —John Greenleaf Whittier

Noah

God remembered Noah and all ... that were
with him in the ark .... (Genesis 8:1)

In the first summer following my graduation from seminary I was invited to speak at a church in San Francisco, and I chose these words as the text for my sermon. My outline was nicely alliterated—Noah as faithful, frail, forgotten—and I was reasonably sure that these words described why God would remember this interesting character in a story from the mists of ancient Hebrew thought. It was a good first-year sermon, and people expressed appreciation.

Recently I revisited the words and wrote another sermon—same outline, even a few of the same illustrations. But my conclusion was the exact opposite. None of the characteristics or actions of Noah had anything to do with why God remembered him.

God remembered because that is the way God is. God's name, Yahweh, usually translated "I Am," can be understood best in modern English to mean "I'll Be Around." God is the one who is there. Remembering the people of his creation is what God does. It is in the very nature of God. What we do or do not do contributes nothing to God's motives. God is simply a caring, loving—remembering—God.

A few weeks before that first sermon I had stood in line waiting to receive my seminary diploma. The man standing in front of me that night turned to me as we waited and said, "I have to tell you a story." Quickly and quietly he told me about a drunken sailor sitting on the steps of a bar in San Diego and of a well-dressed man who dropped a ticket in the sailor's lap, a ticket to a nearby servicemen's center where he could get a meal. He said that the group there was led in singing some Sunday school songs, and there was a simple talk by the well-dressed man about God's love for them. The sailor responded, and his life got turned around that day. "God remembered a drunken sailor," he told me as he turned to go up the steps for his diploma, "and tonight he becomes a preacher. I was that sailor, Mike. We have a good God, don't we!"

It was God's goodness that caused Noah to be remembered. It was God's goodness that found a lost sailor on the streets of San Diego. That same God remembers the faithful, that same mercy finds the weak, that same goodness comes alongside the forgotten in other circumstances, in every place, through every day. God is around, and God is good.

Safeguard

*"(Adam) must not be allowed to reach out his
hand and take also from the tree of life and eat,
and live forever." So the Lord God banished him
from the Garden of Eden. (Genesis 3:22, 23)*

In the north woods of Wisconsin a tiny bunch of fundamentalist believers meets in homes with no more than five or six members to a congregation. The result of several splits in an already small, ultra-conservative denomination, they see themselves as a faithful remnant, true believers clinging fiercely to truth while the rest of the Christian world pursues its fallacies.

Oddly enough, this little collection of house churches donated a substantial sum to the Bible publisher for which I worked, and I paid a call to say thanks and to seek possible further donations. The 93-year old bishop and founder of the group invited me to his home for coffee, conversation and prayer . . . and a lesson about God.

His home was an old two-story house, the central feature of which was a huge, brick oven in an open-hearth kitchen. A low fire burned there night and day and was used for heating the house as well as cooking. The place was a heaven of smells—coffee, the alder wood fire, and the fresh bread he had baked for my visit.

The bishop had one complaint about the project his group had donated to support. It was a children's story Bible newly translated into Russian that included the tale of Adam and Eve being kicked out of the Garden of Eden as punishment for their sin in eating the forbidden fruit. "That's not what the Bible says," he insisted. "God wasn't punishing Adam, he was protecting him. God's way is always grace. Adam had disobeyed, and if he were now to eat also of the tree of eternal life, humans would live forever as sinners. God, who is love, had to preserve us from that fate, so he sent angels to guard the gate to Eden and to keep Adam from disaster."

The bishop had gone so far as to type up his version and tape it on that page of each copy of the book used by the children of his congregations. "When you give that book to the children of Russia, be sure it tells the story the right way," he said gruffly. "They need to know that God is about grace and protection even when they do something wrong."

They say that the sense of smell is the most powerful link we have to memory. Still today the scent of coffee brings to my mind an aged bishop and his fire, and the smell of fresh baked bread recalls the truth of a God concerned to protect—not punish—me.

Evidence

I meditate on all your works and consider what your hands have done. (Psalm 143:5)

A faithful soul from my church called to tell me she read that scientists have found remnants of stone water jars near the town of Cana in northern Israel. It is believed to be the site of Jesus' first miracle, the place where he turned water into wine at a wedding reception. Because there is reason to think these stone fragments are first century in origin, some folks immediately speculated that they may be the very ones in which the water— and then the wine—were contained. "God is out to bring faith to a doubting world," she concluded.

E. J. Carnell, one of my professors in seminary (whose only complimentary remark about any paper I ever wrote for him was: "Neatly typed"), used to tell us that faith "rests in the sufficiency of the evidence." To illustrate, he placed a chair in front of the room and asked if we thought it would bear his weight. We looked at him, looked at the chair, and agreed that it would do so.He explained that our guesses were statements of faith. Though we had not actually seen him sit on the chair prior to expressing our belief that it would hold him, we had seen others sit on similar chairs and thus had accumulated evidence that

59

chairs support people. There was enough evidence at hand for us to have faith in the chair, and so we responded positively. Then, of course, he sat down and confirmed our estimation—and our faith.

Faith in God—like our faith in the professor's chair—is confident trust that rests in the sufficiency of the evidence. It is not just wishful thinking based on optimistic outlooks or positive feelings. Our evidence, however, has nothing to do with a few pieces of first century stoneware. Rather, we consider what God's hands have done in our lives already—as well as in the lives of others. We remember God's past works and conclude that God is alive . . . God is love . . . God is good.

Some years ago other scientists were at work trying to recover what might be remnants of Noah's ark from Mount Ararat in Turkey. Then too there were hopes expressed that success in such a venture would demonstrate the validity of faith in God. But we do not need proof from Cana or Ararat. It is as near to us as the hearts of people who care, the actions of those who trust, the kindness of one who sacrifices for another's sake, the courage of all who persevere.

Now *that* is evidence. Meditate on *that* kind of data and we will move toward faith.

Hiding

Then the man and his wife heard the sound of the Lord God as he was walking in the garden in the cool of the day . . . (and) the Lord God called to the man, "Where are you?" (Genesis 3:8, 9)

When I was a boy my friends and I used to play a game on summer evenings called Washington Poke. It was only a slightly more complex version of Hide and Seek, but it had a ritual to it that made it far superior in our eyes. The person who was "it" stood facing the elm tree on the boulevard while someone drew a frying pan on his or her back. The rest of us, one by one, drew items in the frying pan which we announced solemnly and with no little pride in our imagination and creativity. Then someone would ask, "And who will poke?" Someone jabbed a finger into the middle of the frying pan, and we all scattered, looking for places to hide. The "it" counted to a hundred and began the search, trying to tag us before we could get back to the tree and shout, "Free!"

One evening—maybe we started late or just played too long—the game did not end. Twilight turned to darkness, and I was still crouching in the bushes beside the Pratt's house. I had heard a few shouts of "Free!" but stayed in hiding. Minutes went by—

many of them—with no more noises, no call of "All outs in free!" to signal the end of the game.

Not sure of what to do, but sure that I did not want to be caught, I kept still. Then I heard footsteps and a whispering voice calling my name. It was my dad. "Mike, are you there? Time to come home. Mike, are you there? C'mon home now, it's dark." I was glad to hear that voice. Now I could come out of hiding.

When the Lord God went looking for Adam and Eve in the Garden, it was to rescue them. Many read the story assuming that the Lord had come to punish the guilty, hiding pair. But God's concern that day in Eden was only the welfare of his creation. It was a loving Father who had come to take his children away from the Garden, not as punishment but as protection. They had, according to the Genesis story, sinned by eating of the tree of the knowledge of good and evil. Now they had to be guarded from the possibility of eating also of the tree of eternal life and so living forever as sinful beings.

God is always searching for us, beloved children hiding in our flimsy shelters, hoping the darkness will cover us. How good it is to hear those footsteps, that voice inviting us home.

Pace

*Cast all your anxiety on (God) because he cares
for you. (1 Peter 5:7)*

A generation or so ago Kosuke Koyama wrote a book called *Three-Mile an Hour God*. The title was taken from the approximate distance a healthy person can walk in an hour and suggests that God moves in our lives at our pace.

That is a comforting thought. God does not go too slow or too fast. In times when we are racing along and are surprised that months—not to mention days—have disappeared, we can be sure that God has not lost touch with us. The opposite is also true: when it feels like every minute is an hour and every hour an eternity, God continues to sustain and encourage persons of faith.

At the end of World War II, as Allied soldiers were sweeping across Germany, they often had to go from building to building in a search for weapons and snipers. In one abandoned farm house that was hardly more than a pile of rubble, some soldiers used flashlights to find their way to the cellar. There on a crumbling wall, someone had scratched a Star of David. Beneath it, in rough letters, was this message:

I believe in the sun, even when it does not shine.
I believe in love, even when it is not shown.
I believe in God, even when God does not speak.

Someone believed that God was keeping pace, caring for him or her, even when life was unimaginably difficult. Whether victim or survivor of the Holocaust, this was a person who knew that God walked—or ran—or sat—alongside.

Old Man Peterson (everyone called him that) lived in a run-down nursing home. A member of my first church, he seemed not to care whether I visited him or not, but as a dutiful young pastor, I felt I should occasionally drop in. It was always a brief and perfunctory visit. One day I was in a hurry to finish my required pastoral calls, and I dashed up the stairs and into his room. "Ain't nothin' worth hurryin' for that much," he said. "Come back when you can sit and talk a while."

If we are to be authentic in representing the God of love and mercy to people, we will come alongside them at their pace. Fast or slow, God walks with us. In every way, at any speed at which life is moving for us, God cares. God keeps pace.

Promises

**I have made a vow to the Lord that I cannot
break . . . . (*Judges 11:35*)**

There are some sad stories in the Bible, but none, I think,
sadder than that of Jephthah and his daughter (Judges 11). It has
no redeeming qualities, reflects no mercy, provides no wisdom
or true insight about God. It stands only as an example of what
not to do.

More than eleven hundred years before Christ the leaders of
the Israelite tribes asked Jephthah, a social outcast who had become chief of a fierce band of marauders, to lead them into battle
against the forces of Ammon. He agreed, and in the heat of battle
one day, eager to prove his worth to the people who had previ-
ously rejected him, Jephthah made a vow to God: *If you let me
win this one, Lord, I'll give you the first thing I see come out of my
door on my return home!*

He chased the enemy through twenty towns, won the war
decisively and returned to Israel a hero. The first thing he saw
was his fifteen-year old daughter who, in vibrant, youthful love,
came dancing out the door to greet her conquering father. Com-
pounding one terrible mistake with another, Jephthah assumed
he had to keep his vow and, after allowing her a period of mourn-

65

ing with her friends, had her sacrificed.

If there is anything for us in this story other than disgust at such ignorance and injustice, something more than mourning nameless victims of senseless tragedy, it is the opportunity to consider the nature of the covenant God has made with human beings. A covenant is a promise made by one party, in this case by God. There is no vow we can take, no deal that can be struck, that will strengthen or alter it. A contract requires promises on the part of both sides, but a covenant does not. God's love is unconditional, unqualified, fully effective. God alone sets up the arrangement. There is no need—or room—for our promises in return.

To make vows to God leads only wrong conclusions, for we think we are gaining God's favor if we accomplish certain things, or we judge that we have been inadequate in God's sight if we do not. Neither is true. Neither is possible. My dear dad lived all his life with the burden of his father's promise to God that his only son would be a minister. It was a vow neither father nor son could fulfill, and both were unhappy about it for years.

With God only one promise counts . . . God's own: *I love you just as you are, whatever may come, for as long as you shall live.* Nothing we can offer to do will have any effect on that. Just say thank you.

Risk

In this world you will have trouble. But take
heart! I have overcome the world. (John 16:33)

A nervous man walked into a grocery store in a small town and said to the clerk, "I want to buy all your overripe produce and stale eggs." The clerk gave a knowing grin and commented that the shopper must be planning to go see the new comedian appearing in town that night. The man looked around suspiciously and leaned across the counter. "Not so loud, please!" he whispered. "I *am* the new comedian!"

We try, but there is simply no way to guard against all trouble. We hope, but we cannot make life risk-free. We take sensible precautions, but still there are no guarantees of safety. Thus we do our best to make our house toddler-safe for the visit of our grandson, but he may yet find something to give him a bump and a bruise before it is done. Thus our financial advisor suggests that we get more conservative with our portfolio, but the market still may take a tumble and our investments with it. Thus my neighbor buys a dog to defend his house against possible intruders, only to have the house broken into while he is in Florida and the dog is in a kennel. It is not possible to buy all the stale eggs in town—to make one's world fully safe.

Jesus, of course, spoke of trouble much more serious than these minor irritations. (Sometimes his word is translated "tribulation.") But the way for a person of faith to face trouble of any kind is to remember that it is not the last word. We are meant to live beyond worry for our safety and care for our well-being.

Life is to be spent. Our days are to be used. Those who are happiest and those who accomplish the most seem to be those who live with a sense of abandon, who recognize that trouble will come but that we have resources to overcome it.

Watch people as they walk. Some keep their heads down, eyes on the road, watching for trouble. They seldom trip, rarely get their shoes wet, and nearly always avoid sprained ankles. But they do not see the rainbows, and they miss the light in the faces of their friends. Others hold their heads high, eyes up, watching the world they meet. Occasionally they step in a pot-hole, ruin a good pair of shoes, even break a leg. But they never miss a rainbow, and the faces of their friends are the joy of life to them. Real living goes beyond being cautious.

Faith affirms wisdom's counsel to use common sense. But wisdom affirms faith's commitment not to let trouble—or the fear of it—control life. We belong to one who overcomes the world.

Prophets

In the past God spoke to our forefathers through the prophets at many times and in various ways, but in these last days God has spoken to us by his Son. (Hebrews 1:1, 2)

A man approached me at the start of a worship service and said he had a message he needed to share with the congregation. God had given him a dream concerning our church that he believed to be a prophecy, and he was compelled to deliver it. I said no. This man's history with our congregation told me he simply wanted to agitate people with a confused message of threats, alarm and guilt. Not good news. Not going to happen.

Jesus never brainwashed anyone. He never imposed himself on his followers. He did not threaten, cajole or manipulate. On the contrary, even when he expressed the cost of being a disciple in harshly realistic terms ("take up your cross and follow me"), he left room for choice. It was possible to turn him down without having your arm twisted. When he told a rich man it would be necessary to sell all he had and give the proceeds away prior to becoming a follower, there was no condemnation when the man found the cost too high and turned away.

The time of prophets has gone. The changes God seeks to

bring about in our lives do not happen as a result of coercion from the outside but through a Spirit working from within. The words used to describe that Spirit—Comforter, Advocate, Helper, Counselor—suggest that change of heart is a friendly process. It is a discovery of new life within, a transformation from the inside out. The shouts of the prophets were necessary at one time, and the message they delivered was a much needed one. But in these latter days God has spoken through one who is our brother and whose Spirit moves alongside our own, offering us alternatives, encouragement and hope.

God's Spirit is our friend and, like a good friend, occasionally reminds us of shortcomings we prefer to overlook. Some have called it God's version of tough love. But that Spirit never leaves us empty and alone. It is a Spirit of comfort, of positive direction, of affirmation.

Too often, I think, we have spoken to each other with overtones of the prophets: "Do it right!" . . . "Straighten up!" . . . "Fix what is wrong!"

In these days we are given a gentler message and a better way: "The Spirit is in you!" . . . "The resources are yours!" . . . "Know that you are loved!" . . . "Release what is good!"

Inspiration

*David longed for water and said, "Oh, that
someone would get me a drink of water from the
well near the gate of Bethlehem." (2 Samuel 23:15)*

When, in his old age, ancient Israel's greatest king said he
was thirsty, it was not just any water that he wanted. Only water from the well of Bethlehem would do.

David remembered the early days in his home town when
as a strong young man with big dreams and great visions he
had gone to that well near the city gate. Having worked hard,
he drank deeply. Standing there refreshed, he had looked to a
distant horizon, to what Carl Sandburg called "far lights and
tall rainbows to live by." What David wanted now was that feeling again, that place in life where his heart had been elevated
and his dreams had soared. David's thirst was for inspiration.

Memories of good emotional experiences are among the great
gifts life offers. We long for the return of the high moments, and
often the memory alone brings back the satisfaction they pro-
vided. Occasionally I take a sentimental drive down the elm-lined
street where I grew up, remembering the friends, the ball games,
the newspaper delivery route, the first families to have television, the long summer evenings. The pleasant memories of being

71

young inspire me again, refreshing my heart like water from Bethlehem's well.

Time never destroys. Time builds shrines, memorials in our minds. You and I can go back to a place where we were inspired. Some will fear that it has all been lost, gone with the wind—that you can't go home again. But nothing good, nothing of value, nothing that has ever happened to bless you has been lost. One moment is overlaid by another, one experience succeeded by another and then moved aside until it becomes vague, but if it inspired you once, the memory of it can inspire again.

Remember the teacher who encouraged you. What were her words? Recall the prize you won. How did it feel? Let your thoughts return to the time that special person told you that you were loved. Let the warmth of it move through you again.

If you are thirsty for inspiration, go back. Go back and linger in the experiences that inspired you, for they are clean and good and strong. Drink again from the well of beautiful memories and the spirit that moved you then will return and touch your soul once more.

Good

A city on a hill cannot be hidden . . . . In the same way, let your light shine before (all) . . . .
(Matthew 5:14, 16)

A man from a small village visited a large village and got lodging at the inn. He was awakened in the middle of the night by the loud beating of drums and asked the innkeeper what was happening. Told that a fire had broken out and that the drums were the village fire alarm, he went back to sleep.

In the morning the fire was out, and he went home with news of the great system they had in the large village. "It's wonderful!" he exclaimed. "When fire breaks out, the people beat their drums and before long the fire is out!" The village elders immediately ordered an extra supply of drums and handed them out to every home. Later, when a fire broke out, there was a deafening explosion of drum beats. The people waited expectantly for the flames to subside . . . and waited . . . until their village burned to the ground.

Just as beating drums will not put out a fire, so mere talking will not give light to the world. There comes a time when one must strike a match, press a switch, or raise the torch. A favorite old minister of mine used to say, "It's good to *do* good!" and he always put the emphasis on the "do." There were plenty of us willing to talk about it, enough of us wanting to discuss it, but he was looking for those who would go ahead and *do* it—would actually *be* the city on a hill.

His words came alive to me one night when, as a seminarian, I was required to participate as a worker at a homeless shelter in Chicago. It had always been a source of pride to me that I had come from the family I did, with two grandfathers who were great preachers and churchmen. From them I had inherited an ability to talk about faith and goodness. But I realized as I watched the caregivers doing their work that night that I was seeing people *doing* good. It occurred to me that in the end I will not be asked about my heritage or my theories as to why men and women find themselves in need of shelter from the streets. I will be asked only about how I treated them at that midnight hour when I took my turn ladling soup and handing out bed linen.

A good person is one who does good. It is not enough to know a good person, or to live with one—or even to come from a family full of them. Proximity does not count.

A peddler in Rome approached a visitor on the street and tried to sell him a hen. He boasted that this was a special hen because it was descended directly from the rooster that crowed when St. Peter denied the Lord. "Yes," the visitor said, "but does it lay eggs?" It's good to *do* good.

Presence

(God) is not far from each one of us, for in him
we live and move and have our being. (Acts
17:27, 28)

Joe Garagiola, the television sportscaster, tells the story of a batter who approached home plate in a World Series game and used his bat to make the sign of the cross in the batter's box. Yogi Berra, who was catching, reached over and rubbed out the cross with his mitt, saying, "Why don't we let God just watch this game?"

I respond like Yogi when I hear of impassioned efforts to allow prayer in public schools, of civic leaders and school boards debating the place of God in their communities, and of campaigns in support of judges who want plaques of the Ten Commandments displayed in their courtrooms. None of these has any relevance to the presence of God.

God is in our classrooms when we do education, pursue truth and learn to wonder at the depth and breadth of creation, to marvel at the courage of the human spirit. God is in our courts when we do justice and love mercy. God is in our public buildings when leaders lead with integrity and serve the welfare of the people. God is in us and in what we think and do, not in our symbols or rituals. God is in the middle of things. We find God in our very life and being.

In Samuel Beckett's haunting play *Act Without Words*, a lone actor is seen on a bare stage that is his world. A whistle is heard offstage. The man walks to the wings to investigate but is thrown to the floor. He gets up slowly, confused. The whistle is heard from the other side of the stage, again he searches and again he is thrown down. A series of objects—a tree, boxes, fruit, scissors—appear from above, but each proves useless in providing meaning. Finally the man lies on the stage without hope, no longer even trying to respond to the whistles.

The play suggests to me—though it is likely not what Beckett intended—that God is not found out there (offstage) or up there (dropped from above). God is *in* there, inside our doubting, lonely hearts.

Last spring a small brown finch with a touch of red on her throat worked for a month to build a nest on top of the lamp that lights our deck. She snuggled into it one day, and soon three tiny fuzzy heads were visible. For another few weeks she and her mate airlifted food into that dangerous, human-infested area. Then one afternoon in late July I heard her call from the maple tree at the end of the yard. In a moment the three young ones had flown away to meet her, never to return to their little nest.

God is even on my deck, and I do not need a plaque there to tell me so.

Suffering

As an example of patience in the face of suffering, take the prophets who spoke in the name of the Lord. (James 5:10)

Aunt Marian was the wisest person and most trusted confidant I knew growing up. If a prophet can be described as one who perceives God's will and speaks it in love, then the label belonged to her. The prophet Marian. Though she would have denied the title with a chuckle, many would affirm that she deserved it.

Aunt Marian died some years ago of ALS —"Lou Gehrig's disease." For eight years her heart and will and mind continued strong while she suffered, her body diminished daily by the ravages of the illness. She struggled at first to communicate the simplest messages, and when her speech failed, she would write with increasing difficulty on her yellow pad. Then when her writing failed, she took up a message board, pointing one by one to the letters that spelled out what she wanted to say.

Those messages contained no wasted words. They came only with great labor and so said only what was needed, no more — as a prophet might speak. On more than one occasion when she did not want visitors, the letters she pointed to were *GO AWAY.*

One day I visited and politely, awkwardly, asked her how she was doing. Stupid question —body shriveled, barely able to move, fed through a tube. With twisted finger she jabbed out slowly her response : *BY THE MERCIES OF GOD*. It was something a prophet might say about the way to handle suffering.

Under the roof of the mosque in Hebron in southern Israel, in the middle of the floor, is a circular opening covered by a silver grate. From it is suspended a chain that descends deep into the earth. At the end of the chain a lamp is burning in a cave far below. You are looking into the cave of Machpelah in which is believed to rest the dust of Abraham, the father of faith. You are standing above the place he bought to bury his wife Sarah and where he too was buried. A cool wind blows on your face as you look into that cave, and one feels that the wind of faith, the wind of the ages that touched the prophets, is touching you.

That wind blew through Aunt Marian's home that day as I read her board. May we bear whatever suffering may come our way with the patience of the prophets—by the mercies of God.

Remembering People

There is a destiny that makes us brothers
None goes his way alone.
All that we send into the lives of others
Comes back into our own.
                              —Edwin Markham

People

When he saw the crowds, he had compassion on
them, because they were harassed and helpless....
(Matthew 9:36)

Bob took me to lunch at an exclusive downtown club one day and taught me something I have not been able to lose in the years that have passed since that noon hour. I can still see the table covered with white damask and the sweat slowly rolling down the outside of crystal glasses that were consistently kept full of ice water by attentive waiters.

We were speaking of the church, and I confessed my envy of his position as president of a retail business that could sign paychecks and therefore expect people to do what he wanted. As a pastor, I had to convince and persuade, to listen to a dozen conflicting opinions and then win people over to what I thought we should do.

Bob leaned across the table and brought the palm of his hand down hard on the damask. "No!" he barked, and the water glasses trembled. "It's always about people! It doesn't matter if you're in a profit-making business like I am or church work like you are. Ninety-five percent of all the problems and 95 percent of all the solutions are people!"

A waiter came over and brought the water levels up to the brim again. There may have been a slight grin on his face.

Our problems are people problems. There is no devilish force or alien philosophy or demonic plot out there threatening us. The difficulty is just that we are human and surrounded by other humans. It is that we and they have hearts that get hurt, pride that gets crushed, spirits that are loaded down with guilt and shame. T.S. Eliot once observed that "The desert is not remote in the southern tropics; the desert is squeezed in the tube-train next to you." The desert is in our hearts. The problem is people, harassed and helpless.

And the solutions are people solutions too. There is nothing we can take and nothing to buy. The solution is already in our hearts—respect for ourselves, kindness for others. In Cervantes' *Don Quixote*, Aldonza, a crude woman of the streets, has come to believe that the love this strange knight-errant has shown her is actually real. As he lies dying, she has taken on the *persona* of Dulcinea, the new name he has given her. But, she confesses, love is hard to accept. Beatings and abuse she can tolerate, but his tenderness is almost more than she can bear.

Love is the answer—kindness from the heart, tenderness in the voice—one to another. It is the only thing no one can resist forever. The solution is in us. The solution *is* us. It is always about people.

Silas

Carry each other's burdens, and in this way you
will fulfill the law of Christ. (Galatians 6:2)

Silas called me early on a Saturday evening and said he would pick me up in fifteen minutes. "We have a visit to make," he said. I was a young pastor in my first church, and Silas, a school principal, was chair of the congregation. I knew where we were going.

A few weeks earlier, I had placed signs on the two back pews of our little church that said *Reserved for Parents with Small Children.* There had been some knowing smiles and raised eyebrows when I informed the board. "This will be interesting," someone had remarked. What I had not known—and everyone else did—was that two long time members of the church had sat there, in the same spot, every Sunday for forty years. In fact, they had made it a point to arrive 45 minutes early each week just to be sure they got the end seats in the last pew.

The week that the signs went up, I was told, they had simply made a U-turn and gone back home. I did not want to take the signs down because the church was growing with lots of young families. But neither did I want to lose two veteran—if stubborn—members. They had not returned to church and I had not

83

dared to approach them by the time Silas called.

We drove in silence to Harry's and Florence's house. "Let me handle this," Silas said as we got out of the car and headed up the dreaded sidewalk. We sat in the living room, and Silas did the talking—*all* the talking. He spoke of how our church was growing and emphasized the value of their contributions to our fellowship in the past and how important they, as long time members, were to this increasingly younger congregation. He mentioned how valuable it is to try new things occasionally and to break out of old patterns.

Finally he said, "Harry and Florence, you have a decision to make. Either you'll have to look for another place to sit so we can accommodate families with children, or you may want to consider finding another place to worship. We certainly hope you'll stay with us. Pastor, will you lead us in prayer? Then we'll be on our way."

On the trip home, I was quiet, in awe of the way he had handled conflict. I managed only to say thanks as I got out of the car. Silas grinned and said, "Well, the Bible says we should carry each other's burdens, and I thought I would be the best one to carry this one for you."

A few weeks later, Harry and Florence were back in church—45 minutes early—seated in the third row from the back, just in front of where they had sat for forty years. Silas had carried not only my burden that night, but theirs as well, and we all were able to move on.

Tony

Listen to your father, who gave you life . . . .
(Proverbs 23:22)

On Sunday mornings Dad would wake me early and drive me on my paper route. Sunday papers were too heavy to be carried easily, so he drove slowly down the street, papers stacked in the Ford Fairlane, while I ran back and forth to front doors to make deliveries. It is easy to listen to a father when he helps make your life easier.

There was a time I came home late from playing backyard football on the evening when our family was to attend the grandparents' 50th wedding anniversary party. I was worried that my mother's anger might know no bounds, but it was dad who met me at the back door. "We don't want to be late," he said calmly. "Get your gear off and come to the table for supper." It is comforting to listen to a father when he is a man with a quiet heart.

There was a day when I was fired from a job for the first time. I was in high school and had been working part time at Mac's Men and Boys Clothing. The three weeks there had been boring beyond belief, and so I had asked at the Red Owl grocery store about getting my former job back. Mac heard about my interview, called me in following the Saturday afternoon shift and fired me, saying he needed someone dependable. Mother refused to believe that any son of hers would be fired, and she accused me of quitting. Dad smiled and said, "No dishonor in losing a job. Congratulations on your first time. You'll find a better one." It is encouraging to listen to a father when he trusts you and gives you space.

There was the morning he came to watch me play in the local match play golf tournament. I was losing with three holes to play when I noticed my opponent teeing his ball ahead of the markers—a violation I could use to win that hole. I looked at my dad and asked if he saw what I saw. He put his hand on my shoulder and whispered, "You don't want to win that way. Winning is good, but being a gentleman is better." It enables one to listen to a father when there is wisdom in his counsel.

There was the night I called him to say I had decided to go into the ministry as a career. He was silent for a moment, then asked with a crack in his voice, "I didn't push you into it, did I? There was no pressure from me, right?" Never had we discussed the subject, but he was concerned that he not make the same mistake with me that his father had made with him. So he had to ask, had to be sure. It is a blessing to listen to a father when his goal is to set you free.

They say those who have had a kind and loving father (or father-figure in their lives) have an easier time believing in the goodness of God. It has certainly been that way for me. Thanks, Dad.

Andrei

Create in me a pure heart, O God, and renew a
steadfast spirit within me. (Psalm 51:10)

It was a hot, humid morning in Yalta, Crimea, the southern point of Ukraine. I was sitting, perspiring, on the curb of a tourist parking area near Livadia Palace, once a summer residence of Tsar Nicholas II and site of an historic conference of Allied leaders toward the end of World War II. My heart rate was well over 200 beats per minute.

For over forty years I had lived with SVT, an electrical problem of the heart that caused it periodically to shift into high gear. Doctors had assured me that, although producing anxiety and discomfort, SVT was not life-threatening. Episodes were very occasional, sometimes one in a month, sometimes none at all in three years, and they lasted from thirty seconds to thirty minutes. On this morning in Yalta, however, an hour had passed, and my heart was still racing.

A friend called an ambulance, and within minutes the world's oldest panel truck, brown with a red cross painted on it, pulled up. Soon I was being wheeled into Yalta's hospital which from my gurney looked something like my garage. I was put into the hospital's version of Intensive Care where, after an hour—in a moment, just as these episodes always ended—my heart switched back into its normal rhythm.

I started to climb out of the bed, but a husky voice with a Russian accent told me to lie down, please. It was a doctor whose nametag I could make out as Andrei. "What is the matter with your American doctors?" he demanded to know. "They know very well how to take care of this problem and have the equipment to do it! We can only read of such things! You must tell your doctors you need radial ablation!" (In fairness, my doctors *had* mentioned such a possibility, but I had opted for more conservative treatment.)

A month later I was in a U.S. hospital for the procedure. It took two hours, and I was home the same evening. There have been no SVT episodes since. Dr. Andrei, with knowledge but no resources—with determination and no hesitation—changed the state of things for me and my heart.

What happened that day near the Tsar's palace causes me to reflect on the other heart-fix we all need. I remember with gratitude the people in my life who have made that message as clear and forthright as Dr. Andrei did concerning SVT. Pure hearts.... Renewed spirits . . . . May the word be heard from Yalta to the ends of the earth.

Joe

*Have you entered the storehouses of the snow or
seen the storehouses of the hail? (Job 38:22)*

A long line of mourners made its way up the hill of the cem-
etery outside of town. It was my first pastorate and one of my
first funerals. The ground was soft under our feet as we pro-
cessed through the last traces of April snow. I made a comment
to the effect that spring was coming too late, and I was immediately and gently chastised by Joe Topolewski, one of the
pallbearers behind me. "All in God's time, Pastor," he said, "all
in God's time." And quoting Job, he asked me, "Have you entered the storehouses of the snow?" He meant, as Job did, that it
is not our place to question God.

It was so like him. Joe was a school teacher and directed the
church choir. But he suffered from an unknown physical ailment
that was the center of his and his family's life. We all thought, as
he did, that it was a mental disorder because he was subject to
delusions and episodes of strange behavior that seemed to have
no other explanation. Medication had been prescribed, and when
he took it, the symptoms subsided, but he was left moving slowly,
without his usual energy, creativity or lively wit.

So Joe hated the pills and frequently decided not to take them.

He made it a spiritual issue, as he did the coming of the spring. All in God's time, he thought. But if God was going to heal him, he reasoned, God would want him to prove his faith by not taking medication. Inevitably I would get a phone call that Joe had had another episode and was in the hospital, and then he would be back on the pills for a time.

Fifteen years later I returned to the city for an anniversary and spent a few minutes going through the memorial book in the church's foyer. The name leaped out at me: *Joe Topolewski, died April 25, 1978.* I wondered if there had been any traces of snow on the ground that day as they had walked up the hill to lay Joe's body into the ground. They told me an autopsy had revealed he died of a brain tumor, surely the cause of his delusions and odd behavior.

There are no answers, of course, as to why such things happen, or why they happen to us and those we love. We have not entered the storehouses of the snow or seen the reservoirs of the hail. Like Joe—and like Job—we keep putting one foot in front of another even when the ground feels uncertain under our feet. And, though we do not separate medicine from faith, we trust in God's time, believing God will sustain us through whatever may come.

Dwight

*Do everything you can to help Zenas the lawyer
and Apollos on their way and see that they have
everything they need. (Titus 3:13)*

My mother had an older brother whom she did not like very
much. Her reasons were her own, and I had no basis on which
to question them. There were times, apparently, when my behavior, or maybe my appearance, brought him to mind. When
she was unhappy with me she would say in disgust, "You're
just like your Uncle Dwight!" It was never a compliment.

Uncle Dwight lived in southern California, a long way from
us, and I do not remember meeting him until I was a college
student. I had made a trip to Los Angeles for the Rose Bowl
game and stayed at his house. Like him, I loved books, and the
3,000 volume library of theology books in his home was the most
wonderful I had ever seen. His wit and easygoing hospitality
charmed that young college student, and I immediately had a
new favorite uncle. I wanted to be like Uncle Dwight!

Two years later as newlyweds—and with a three month old
baby—my wife and I moved to Los Angeles where I was to enroll
in seminary. We had no apartment lined up, no job and—arriving
in town with three dollars in our pockets—no money.

Uncle Dwight and Aunt Patty invited us to live with them until we could find an apartment and to store our belongings in their garage until we moved into our own place a month later. He gave me his gasoline credit card to use for the next year. As often as we came for dinner on Sundays (steaks at Johnny's) for the next three years, he never once let me buy a meal.

And there was that day twenty years later when a truck pulled up to my office door with 82 boxes of books. Uncle Dwight, long retired and in poor health, had decided to give me his entire library. A note inside the first box said, "Every good preacher needs a good library. Use what has value and throw away the chaff. There will be some things here to help you along the way." If only I were generous enough to be like Uncle Dwight!

When we offer people what they need and give a hand to help them along the way, we are living life as it ought to be lived. If someone were to tell me today I am just like Uncle Dwight, I would take it as a compliment.

Yes

Since we are surrounded by such a great cloud of witnesses, let us throw off everything that hinders . . . , and let us run with perseverance the race marked out for us. (Hebrews 12:1)

"Yes" may be the most wonderful word in the English language. We love . . . and we need . . . to hear that word, in big moments or small. It is what our hearts ache for after asking, "Daddy, may I go with you?" or "Would you go with me to the movies?" or "Will you marry me?" Yes, we'll take it. Yes, we'll join. Yes, we'll go with you. Yes, you may. Yes, I love you. Yes, I remember you. *Yes.*

People of faith live by what they affirm, not by what they deny. To be positive makes us more likely to find harmony with what God wants to accomplish in the world and in us. It keeps us from having to be protective of boundaries and defensive about choices. It prevents us from having always to be on guard. I am constantly looking for people who say yes to life. I want them around me. I want to be such a person to them.

Carlyle Marney said that people of faith always have with us our "balcony people." He suggested that we imagine that the room in which we are sitting is the inside of our minds and that to one side of the room is a balcony filled with people who are cheering for us. We recognize their faces, for these are the people we have encountered who have inspired us, made us feel that we are capable of more than we think. Some are no longer living, but their inspiration remains for their "Yes" never dies. Its importance to us is never diminished.

My "balcony people" include spouse and parents and siblings and children. Front row seats in the balcony for them! They include the man who first challenged me to consider a call to ministry, the seminary professor who made me believe I could preach well and the church chairperson who taught me how to be a pastor-leader of a congregation. Front row seats for them all! They said "Yes."

I have been naming my balcony people lately as faces come to mind and their encouragement comes to memory. I add the friends who went—and go—through difficult times with me and incidental contacts that have cheered me along the way. I give thanks for that great cloud of witnesses, a full balcony. May I also be one who says "Yes" to others as they run with perseverance the race marked out for them!

Kiril

I am unworthy—how can I reply to you? I put
my hand over my mouth. I spoke once, but I
have no answer—twice, but I will say no more.
(Job 40:4, 5)

Kiril approached me at the end of an evening visit to a youth center in Kostroma, Russia and asked if I would talk to him. His halting English made me think he wanted simply to practice his conversational skills. After a few minutes of small talk, Kiril said, "May I ask you to tell your experience?" I wondered if he meant something about my faith or professional life. "How do you raise children?" he asked. "What does a husband do? What does it mean to be a man?"

Kiril was the only child of a military officer and his wife. Born in the far east of Russia, he was nine years old when his father died of alcoholism. He and his mother moved to small mining village, but economic conditions soon worsened for them, and they found an apartment in the Siberian city of Omsk.

When Kiril was thirteen, his mother became ill (he was not clear on the nature of her ailment) and was hospitalized. For months no one knew that he was alone and taking care of himself. Finally a teacher learned what was going on and helped him enter a military boarding school. From there he was sent to Kostroma—where his mother was being kept—to attend a trade school.

Now seventeen and living in a dormitory, apparently without male role models in his life, he was wondering what it meant to be a man. And he was entrusting the privilege of offering an answer—in the ten minutes before the center closed—to me.

I did not know if I was doing the right thing (who is sufficient for such moments?), but I decided to speak as if I knew. He wanted clear answers, not discussion and more questions.

"A good man," I said, "forgives his parents for things they can no longer do anything about, and then decides to get on with making as good a life as possible." I told him about love for one's family, about using one's energy and skill on things that matter in life, about perseverance in the face of obstacles, and about a faith that God has a purpose for him in this world. I cautioned him never to strike a woman or a child, not to let alcohol take over his life as it had his father's, and always to seek the company of friends who shared these values.

The doors were shut, and Kiril walked off into the darkness. I felt like Job: *I am unworthy—how can I reply to you?* I crossed the street with my hand over my mouth but also with a sense that I had been honored above most men in Kostroma that night.

Grandpa

Shall not the judge of all the earth do right?
(Genesis 18:25)

My grandfather was a thunder-voiced, take-no-prisoners preacher who apparently had few doubts about the will of God and no questions about the fate of those who did not submit to it. As a grandfather, however, he was gentle and kind. His pulpit *persona* was left behind when we, his large brood of grandchildren, were crawling around his fascinating library (imagine, an antique typewriter with black and red ribbon!) or combing his silver hair.

He continued to teach Bible classes on prophecy and the second coming of Christ ("that glad morning" he called it)—his favorite subject—long after his retirement. His charts on the Book of Revelation adorned the wall behind him in the classroom of the old church one day when I heard him say something that still rings in my heart.

The lesson was on Judgment, which he portrayed as all persons standing before the God of Creation to receive word of their eternal destiny. Hellfire is fearful to describe and discomforting to consider, and Grandpa usually did both at some length. His own children had spoken of having hidden behind the pillars of the sanctuary when he had preached on this subject in the old days.

But on this day he paused, then stopped, with tears in his eyes. "I wonder," he said, "if in the end God, whose love touched even this immigrant farm boy in the cotton fields of Texas, will open the door to all." There was a long silence. "How could love do otherwise?" he asked quietly.

My grandfather, the greatest Swedish-American evangelist and teacher of prophecy of his time, was wondering at the age of 84 about the possibility of Universalism.

Dear Grandpa,

I wrote today about that time I heard you wonder out loud if God might, in the end, save all people. There is after all, you said, no limit to his love and no end to his compassion. God is love, and love is patient, as you were patient with us children who loved to make a playground of your beautiful old library.

As I look at that question late in my own life and ministry, I believe, as you did, that none will be condemned for failing to respond to a message they did not know or could not hear. No one will shake a fist in God's face and say, "Unjust!" The Judge of all the earth will surely do what is right. But I believe that some, knowing all the options, still will say, "No, thank you. I do not wish to be part of your family. I choose to live forever alone." And because Love is patient, permitting its children to make their own choices—even bad ones—God will allow the beloved to take his leave, to go her way. What do you think?

By the way, I'm a grandpa now too. See you on that glad morning!

Michael

Imposter

The Lord abhors dishonest scales, but accurate weights are his delight. (Proverbs 11:1)

Photographs of me almost always turn out to be of some imposter who has jumped in front of the camera at just the right moment. He is given away by imperfections (especially ears and nose) that obviously could not belong to me. So I was not surprised to see that same face in the proofs of a photograph I had taken in Chicago some years ago.

Ralph was a photographer who had a small studio on the north side of the city, its window filled with portraits of people well known in the neighborhood (none of them the imposter). He listened patiently to my complaints about each proof and thoughtfully offered me another sitting. I apologized for the inconvenience, and he assured me it was no problem. "I often have to do that for my Pharisees," he said.

Pharisee is a Bible term that is never a compliment, so I asked him what he meant. "Pharisees," he said, "are customers who want pictures to flatter them. They're not comfortable in front of a camera, so they're not satisfied with what it shows them. They can't just say 'Here I am' and accept themselves the way others see them. They want the hairline lowered, wrinkles removed or color added to the cheeks." (I decided not to ask about ears and noses.) "And they usually want second sittings."

Strangely enough, several of the proofs suddenly began to look quite a bit more like me, and I found one that would do nicely for my purposes.

Fritz Kreisler, a great violin virtuoso and composer of the 20th century, was so unsure of himself and the way others would receive his music that he attributed his original works to little known composers of the past. He performed these works in concert with the explanation that he had found them as manuscripts in old libraries and edited them for performance. It was not until his sixtieth birthday, by which time his reputation had been firmly established, that Kreisler dared to reveal his secret. The music was actually his own!

It is refreshing to find folks who can just be themselves. They live using honest scales. Neither Pharisee nor fraud, they are comfortable in their own skin, content with their own talents and tolerant of their own imperfections. They approach life with accurate weights and are able to accept what others see so well— the truth about themselves.

Ethel

*Greater love has no one than this, than that he
lay down his life for his friends.* (John 15:13)

Aunt Ethel, my mother's oldest sister, was a warm, hospitable woman who opened her home to me during my senior year of high school, allowing me to graduate with my class after my parents had moved following a job transfer. A witty, wise and gracious person, she was also dying of breast cancer.

She often visited her dad, my grandfather, a widower and also in frail health. I witnessed a conversation between them on a gray November afternoon at a time when we in the family suspected that each of them had no more than a few months to live. As a very young man, I had certainly heard nothing quite like it before, and I have seldom—if ever—heard the likes of it since. It showed me something about love I have not been able to let go.

"Dad," Aunt Ethel, said, "I'm praying that you will die before I do. It isn't right for a parent to have to bury a child, and I don't want you to have to grieve for me."

"No, my beloved daughter," Grandpa replied, using that affectionate expression for his children that he reserved for the most solemn moments, "you must go before me. With all you've been through, it isn't right that you should have to stand at my grave." They laughed through their tears as they realized that love was causing each to want the other to die first.

We have it wrong when we make life the highest value. Those who argue the difficult matters of ethics and morality in our time (pro-life vs. abortion rights, stem cell research, physician-assisted suicide) are not persuasive when they build their cases making life the most precious commodity. Life is not the highest value.

Love is the highest value. Aunt Ethel and my grandfather understood that and revealed it in words of mutual care, shared while they sat laughing and weeping in one another's arms in his living room that day.

Grandpa, of course, had the last word. Aunt Ethel died on Christmas Eve that year, and it was left to him to mourn her passing. A few months later he too was gone. I have no doubt she was waiting to greet him just inside the gates of pearl.

If a willingness to lay down one's life for a friend is the greatest love, surely a profound desire that the beloved be spared the pain of grief is a close second.

Rosie's

(Jesus asked,) "Which of these three do you think was a neighbor to the man who fell into the hands of robbers?" The expert in the law replied, "The one who had mercy on him." Jesus told him, "Go and do likewise." (Luke 10:36, 37)

Bridges are favorite places for me. The caveman who first threw a log into a stream so he could make whatever lay on the other side part of his experience of life had a great idea. I first fell in love with bridges when we lived by a lazy creek crossed by a railroad trestle. My friend and I would hang from the mammoth wooden beams under the bridge as a diesel locomotive crossed overhead and feel the whole world tremble.

I have discovered many other bridges since. A plane is a bridge that gets me across to Los Angeles in three hours or to Moscow in eleven. My car is a bridge that spans the distance to church in fifteen minutes or to the airport in thirty. My phone is a bridge enabling me to go to my sister's house in Denver in seconds (a trip I do not take often enough, I know). The bridge was a great invention.

Years ago, while living in Chicago, I was invited to speak on a Sunday evening in a small church in Wisconsin. Wanting to be sure to be on time, I arrived two hours early and found the door of the church locked. A quarter of a mile back and across the highway was a little roadhouse restaurant and bar called Rosie's Place. From the outside it seemed to have a warm glow about it, and it certainly looked better than sitting in my car until the church opened.

It was like a family gathering inside, with one general conversation going on rather than many private ones. I ordered a sandwich and tried to keep my head down, but they spotted me. "Where you from? Travelin' through?" When I said I was going to speak at the church that night, the conversation moved to people they had known who went to that church, or used to. There was talk of one who had died years before in a boating accident ("terrible thing!").

After an hour of enjoying the atmosphere, I went to the cash register to pay my bill. The waitress taking my money asked the crowd, "Anyone gonna hear the preacher tonight?" There were some chuckles, and she grinned and said to me, "Maybe if the likes of them came in here a bit more often, preacher, the likes of us might go over there. You tell 'em Rosie said so."

That night I talked to the church people about bridges, about the need to build one across that highway to Rosie's Place. Neighbors are people who build bridges to their neighbors. Rosie said so. Jesus did too.

Sharing Moments

*There is a tide in the affairs of men
Which, taken at the flood, leads on to fortune;
Omitted, all the voyage of their life
Is bound in shallows and in miseries.*
                    —William Shakespeare

Moments

The sun stopped in the middle of the sky and delayed going down about a full day. There has never been a day like it before or since. (Joshua 10:13, 14)

Early in my high school years I played one season of junior varsity basketball. Games were scheduled just before varsity contests, and the night we played our biggest rival, the mighty Warriors of Hopkins High, the stands, normally empty for JV games, were filled as fans came early for the feature to follow.

Our game was close throughout, and the crowd got excited— something rarely seen at a JV game. The rivalry was being played out even between junior varsities. We were tied at the end of regulation time, and because the varsity squads were ready to take the floor, the JV coaches agreed we would play sudden-death overtime, with the first team to score two points to be the winner.

Within seconds of the start of overtime I was fouled and awarded two free throws. The fans were cheering as I stepped to the free throw line, knees knocking. I had never been center stage in such an atmosphere.

I eyed the basket and released the ball with too much force, panicked at the thought of embarrassing myself by missing the basket altogether. The ball slammed against the backboard and rebounded down through the net. Sheer luck. A freight train of noise roared through the place, followed by a hush so complete l could hear my teeth chatter.

Trembling but determined to make the second shot more graceful, I managed to send it up toward the basket, a little too high and slightly to the right.

There are occasions in life when time seems to stand still. The sun stops in the sky, the moon lingers over the lake, a pendulum hesitates, a basketball hangs in midair. The world paused in its turning when dressed in a tuxedo I stood at the foot of the aisle and saw my bride appear in the doorway. Life went into slow motion when I stepped on to a stage to receive my graduate degree. Time froze when my old Chevy began to slide across a snowy highway and I saw the faces of the people in the front seat of the car coming at me. The clock never moved when I walked into the hospital room at Mayo Clinic to say goodbye to my dying dad. You have had them too—powerful moments when the sun stands still and life is experienced as a still photograph.

Slowly, gently, the ball landed on the rim and began to bounce—ever so slowly—from one side to another. It bounced and bounced until it lost its desire, then began to roll, two full circuits of the rim, came up for air and lingered for a moment— or for an eternity—in the silence of a breathless gym, and fell through the net. We had won.

Whether meeting the Warriors of Hopkins or, like Joshua, the warriors of the Amorite kings, a soul we love or one we have never seen before, some moments are unlike any other before or since.

Music

We are hard pressed on every side, but not crushed; perplexed, but not in despair. (2 Corinthians 4:8)

The internet carried the story of a November night in 1995 when Itzhak Perlman, the violinist, came on stage at Avery Fisher Hall in New York for a concert. Perlman, who was stricken with polio as a child, has braces on both legs and walks with crutches, and just getting on stage is no small achievement for him. He refuses help, and to see him move so slowly, painfully, is an unforgettable sight.

Majestically, Perlman reached his chair, put his crutches on the floor, and went through the laborious process of unclasping the braces, tucking one foot back and extending the other forward. The audience, familiar with his ritual, sat quietly and reverently through it all. Finally Itzhak Perlman picked up his violin and nodded to the conductor. All was ready.

Then, disaster struck. A few bars into the concerto, one of the strings on his violin broke. The snap could be heard across the concert hall, as clear as a gunshot. There was no mistaking what that sound meant, no mistaking what the world's premier violinist had to do—put the clasps on again, straighten his legs,

109

pick up the crutches and limp off stage—either to replace the string or to find another violin. Instead, Perlman stopped, closed his eyes, waited a moment, then nodded to the conductor again. The orchestra began, and he played from where he had left off.

Everyone knows that you cannot play a concerto for violin with just three strings, but on that night, Itzhak Perlman refused to know that. Those who heard it said he appeared to be modulating, recomposing the piece in his head . . . and they never experienced music played with such passion, power and purity. Some said it sounded like he was re-tuning the strings to get new sounds from them that they had never made before—or playing that invisible fourth string.

When he finished, there was silence for a long moment, and the audience rose as one, cheering, applauding—roaring its appreciation for what he had done. Perlman wiped the perspiration from his brow, raised his bow to silence the crowd, and said in a quiet, pensive tone, "You know, sometimes it's the artist's task to find out how much music you can still make with what you have left." He fastened his braces, picked up his crutches, and limped off stage.

Life is about making music . . . first with all we have been given, and when that is no longer possible, to make music with what we have left. It is to live in the present, to believe in ourselves, to overcome obstacles, and to trust the power . . . and the spirit . . . that is within us all.

Trust

*Trust in the Lord with all your heart and lean
not on your own understanding. (Proverbs 3:5)*

The nineteenth century French tightrope walker known as
Blondin came to America and announced that he would be the
first to cross the gorge below Niagara Falls on a tightrope. On
the afternoon of June 30, 1859 the rope was in position, and
Blondin started the trip that was to make history. Thousands of
incredulous spectators lined both sides of the falls.

At one point this world-famous aerialist paused to lower a
line to the Maid of the Mist, pull up a bottle and sit down for a
bit of refreshment. Later he did a back somersault. The crowd
cheered frantically and demanded more. Blondin, never content
merely to repeat a performance, in subsequent weeks crossed
again on a bicycle . . . then on stilts . . . then blindfolded and
pushing a wheelbarrow. On one trip he carried a small stove
and stopped to cook an omelet. On another he had his hands
and feet manacled. "Do you trust me?!" he shouted to the ador-
ing crowd, and the people roared back their faith that he could
do anything. "All right, then, who will get on my back and cross
with me?" Silence. They did not trust him *that* much.

So Harry Colcord, Blondin's unfortunate manager, was chosen to ride and one day in August found himself high above Niagara Falls on the back of a daredevil determined to carry out this ultimate test of skill and stamina. According to Colcord, the trip was a nightmare. The wind was stronger than anticipated, and in the less stable center section the pair swayed violently. Blondin was fighting for their lives and began to run to reach the first guy wire. As he attempted to steady himself, that guy wire broke, and once more they were swaying dangerously. Again he ran for the next one, and when they reached it, Blondin gasped for Colcord to get down. Six times in all Colcord had to dismount to allow Blondin to regain his strength, until they reached at last the Canadian shore.

Colcord later recalled that what had saved them from disaster that day was that he had obeyed Blondin's shouts to him at the height of the danger: "Harry, out here you and I are one. When I sway, you sway with me. We must be one!"

In our search for happiness, as in our struggle to overcome the difficult moments of life, our tendency is often to want to wrestle with higher powers. We do not really trust God but want to lean on our own wisdom and devices. Only to the degree that we are able to allow God's way to become our own—to sway with God in the gale above the abyss, to make our will one with God's—do we find contentment in the journey and, ultimately, safe arrival at home.

Connection

I see people; they look like trees walking around.
(Mark 8:24)

A blind man received his sight in an encounter with Jesus, but people looked to him like walking trees. He lacked discernment. He was unable to distinguish persons from things. Sometimes a second miracle—a further healing—is necessary to make us truly whole.

I sat in my favorite chair thirty-plus years ago and our then four-year old son climbed up on my lap. He was carrying several of his well-worn books and snuggled into the familiar wedge between my hip and the soft arm of the chair.

We started to read, but my mind was somewhere else—a meeting I had had that day, a chapel service to plan for tomorrow, the ball game that would be on television in an hour or two—just the stuff of my life. After a while, in the distance I became aware of sticky fingers on my cheeks turning my head to the side and of a child's voice insisting, "Daddy, look at me. Daddy, look at me."

I let my head be turned, and I saw again the face of our little boy. What had seemed to be an inconvenient distraction from the things that mattered to me came again into true focus—shin-

113

ing eyes, matted hair and a little grin that said, "Gotcha!" It was not reading that he wanted, but Daddy. The book was only a means to make the connection.

We are less than whole when we see our children as distractions, our spouses as providers. They might as well be trees walking. The miracle of relationship is incomplete when we see a colleague as a problem, a boss as a barrier, or an employee as a tool. A client is not just an appointment and a student is more than a name or number. They are people, and the degree to which we are unable or unwilling to see them as such is the degree to which we need second miracles.

People are not things as surely as trees do not walk. Every connection we make with another person—a real live human being—marks another miracle, another of the continuing blessings of life.

Angels

Do not forget to entertain strangers, for by so doing some people have entertained angels unaware. (Hebrews 13:2)

Many years I stood in the Detroit airport waiting for a visiting missionary and his companion, the president of a large church body in Congo, who were to speak at our church. The flight from Green Bay had been delayed by nearly an hour. When it finally arrived, the first person off the plane—late middle age, business suit, glasses, short, full of energy—rushed over to the gate agent and asked about his connecting flight to New York. As he started walking, then trotting, down the concourse, I had a vague feeling that I recognized him.

The second man off the plane—a large man, black, also in a suit—had a sense of insecurity that told me this was Reverend Joseph, the African I had been waiting for. I introduced myself and asked about Frank, the missionary. Reverend Joseph, who spoke no English at all, handed me a note from Frank indicating that he had been bumped from the overcrowded flight and would be on the next plane. Two hours later we picked up Frank, and as we drove to the hotel, the story unfolded—Joseph speaking, Frank interpreting for me.

Reverend Joseph had been seated in first class next to a very nice man who helped him through the entire flight. The stranger had noticed Joseph reading his Bible and immediately took out his own. Through hand signals and nods they had agreed to read together, line by line, each in his own language, so they could share something despite the communication barrier. They read the book of Ephesians as they flew across Lake Michigan.

Frank said, "I wish I knew that man's name so I could thank him for taking such good care of you." Joseph's eyes lit up, and he pulled a business card from his pocket. Frank took a look at it and handed it to me. The name on the card was Norman Vincent Peale—America's most famous preacher and author of *The Power of Positive Thinking*. No wonder I had recognized that man in the airport!

Later I wrote to Dr. Peale to tell him the story. I thought he might like to know something about the stranger who had been seated next to him and to whom he had been such a help. Dr. Peale responded warmly that he too had been blessed and suggested that they had been "angels unaware" to one another on that plane.

I want to be tuned in to the angels nearby—the people, even strangers, whom God seats next to me and who offer the comfort and encouragement I need at just that moment . . . and those for whom I am the angel, who need the blessing I can give to them.

Mysteries

(We are) born to trouble as surely as sparks fly upward. (Job 5:7)

A *Peanuts* cartoon showed Charlie Brown, pitching his baseball team to another disaster, having a conference on the mound with Schroeder, his catcher. Suffering always seemed to be Charlie Brown's lot, and he asked Schroeder why he had to go through this again. From inside his mask the little catcher responded with words from the mouth of one of Job's friends who was also trying to console him in his suffering: "Man is born to trouble as surely as sparks fly upward."

We wonder why things go wrong. Occasionally we see reasons—poor planning, lack of leadership, bad decisions. But most often we have to be content with not knowing. Even if there are specific causes, they are not known to us. And in many cases there are no reasons to be found. Things just happen, and the mysteries of why live after them.

Chuck was a well known character in the small town in southern Minnesota where my parents used to live. He drove a bronze-colored '55 Chevy that everyone knew on sight. So Taillight Teddy, the local state highway patrolman, had no trouble knowing who it was that slowed down one day on the Hastings cutoff and threw a gunny sack into a field. He had been parked on a gravel road watching for speeders when Chuck's Chevy made its drop.

After Chuck had driven away, Teddy investigated. He found a litter of newborn kittens in the sack. Putting kittens and sack into the back seat of his patrol car, Teddy turned on the red lights and started back for town. He headed straight for the house where he knew the bronze Chevy belonged and left the kittens on the back porch.

Months later in the downtown pizza parlor, Chuck spoke in awe of how cats could always find their way home and of how he had once taken some kittens "to give them away" and driven the twenty miles back home only to find them purring in the sunlight of his back porch. "And I drove fast too," he said. "The only one who passed me was Taillight Teddy chasing some guy on the rip-rap north of town." Chuck might have lived out his days without ever knowing what happened had it not been for a few of his friends, our sides aching with laughter, who could not hold back the secret.

Sometimes there are no reasons for things—or none known to us. They are just there, and we are bound to go through them. What we do with things that we cannot explain—the trust, courage and determination we find to live with the mysteries of life—shapes our character.

Announcer

*I will not venture to speak of anything except
what Christ has accomplished through me.*
(Romans 15:18)

As a family we had gone to the old Union Depot in downtown Minneapolis to greet my grandparents who were returning from an extended trip to Sweden. (Those were the days when one traveled to Europe by ship and the return from New York to the Midwest was by train.) I was nine years old and fascinated by the cavernous marble hall that was Union Depot. The acoustics alone made the atmosphere exciting, every sound echoing endlessly in the ear.

From time to time a voice came over the public address system announcing the trains: *Now boarding from Track 7, the North Coast Limited, for Fargo, Bismarck, Billings and all points west. All aboard, please.* If only I could get on that train! Imagine the adventure of visiting Billings and all points west! I looked around the enormous waiting room to see if I could find where the voice came from that announced such a thrilling possibility.

Uncle Ted noticed my curiosity about the voice and motioned to me to follow him. He led me toward the ticket counter and silently pointed to an office behind it. Through the small win-

119

dow I could see a man seated at a desk, a microphone in front of him. I watched as he made the next announcement, feeling as though I knew a secret. "It's not such a great job," my uncle said with a laugh. "He's probably never even been to any of those places he talks about."

That poor man, I thought. It must be hard to welcome people aboard for all those wonderful destinations—from the plains to the mountains, from the mountains to the sea—and all the while have no more of a view for himself than the back side of a row of ticket agents!

Some of us work in a world of words. We are responsible to write or speak or announce with an expectation that some will get on board. We invite and encourage—even persuade—people to consider new destinations and different directions for their lives. It may sound at times like we have been to all the wonderful places of which we speak—that the attitudes and choices and perspectives we commend to others have been our own all along. In fact, some of us fall well short of accomplishing the good things we proclaim.

May we be more than track announcers, merely inviting others to the very places we ourselves would like to be. All aboard!

Prosthesis

Since you have taken off your old self with its
practices and have put on the new self . . . clothe
yourselves with compassion, kindness, humility,
gentleness and patience. (Colossians 3:9, 10, 12)

A church which I served as interim minister had several faithful participants who were members of a motorcycle gang. The president of the gang ("not a club—a *gang!*" he insisted) was a cheerful, outspoken man with a huge mustache who spoke freely of his faith. With his jeans and biker boots on it was impossible to tell that he wore a prosthesis on the lower half of one leg, the result of a motorcycle accident some years before.

One Sunday we held an outdoor service and picnic on the expansive lawn of the church, and the gang of bikers decided to attend. We were treated to the dramatic picture of a line of Harleys coming up the road and turning into the church parking lot. The riders mingled freely with the congregation and joined the people seated on the grass as we began the service.

A young girl sitting near the gang leader noticed that one of his distinctive boots had a kind of pole sticking out of it where a leg ought to be, and she decided to investigate further. He was amused by her interest, and slowly, in the middle of a worship song, he raised the leg of his jeans and unbuckled the prosthesis at the knee. He removed it and set it beside him without a word. The girl took one look at the leg on the grass and ran for her laughing mother, leaping into her arms, all the while pointing breathlessly behind her at the man who could take off his leg.

The gang leader told me later that he occasionally used his artificial limb in speaking about faith to students and youth groups. He reminded me that in faith we have taken off our old selves with its practices. To demonstrate, he would remove and discard the prosthesis which represented selfishness, telling lies and using crude language. He then strapped on a second artificial limb, the one he used for walking (the first had his riding boot permanently attached and was just for biking). The new leg represented kindness, caring and patience—the positive values we do well to practice each day.

They say it takes just 21 days to develop a new habit. Take off the apathy and buckle on love. Pull off the skepticism and strap on trust. Let go of the hostility and try on a bit of humility. Erase the hard edge and put on some gentleness. Repeat for 21 days. There may be a lot of old boots lying around in the grass.

They will not be missed.

Planks

**Why do you look at the speck of sawdust in
your brother's eye and pay no attention to the
plank in your own eye?** (Matthew 7:3)

In an effort to improve my speaking and leadership skills, I
occasionally ask colleagues and friends for feedback. My questions are focused, centering on affirmation of specific skills and
identification of shortcomings that can be addressed and overcome. Critical comments are okay as long as they show
perception and sensitivity. After all, I asked for them.

In a recent such review, one person commented that he would
like to hear me talk more about what is right and wrong and to
warn people, especially youth, to avoid certain things (he was
not specific about what they were). He was right in noticing that
I seldom do that, and in fact I have taken pains to avoid doing so
for many years. Maybe he would have liked my speaking meth-
ods better in my younger days. I was fairly certain of my opinions
then and direct in expressing them . . . until I met Joe Bayly.

Joe Bayly was vice president of a publishing company and
himself a wonderful writer. The father of a large family, he and
his wife suffered tragedies in losing several of their kids at young
ages, and he wrote powerfully about grief and God's grace.

Joe spoke in our seminary chapel service one day only a few months after the death of his son, a student at Swarthmore College, in an automobile accident. He told of having to drive from Chicago to Philadelphia to clean out his son's dormitory room. He knew he would find it exactly as his son had left it, certain that he would be returning there in a few days. Pausing frequently as the emotions revisited him in that seminary chapel, Joe spoke of emptying drawers and opening boxes. "And I want you to know that there was nothing there which my son would have been ashamed to let me see," he concluded, and he sat down.

No reference was made to our lives or question asked about our rooms. None was necessary. I knew my dad would not have been able to say the same about my room that day, and I went home and cleaned it out—cleaned it up—that very morning.

My talk to the youth group at church the following Sunday was a lot softer, I know, and it has been that way for me in the forty years since. It is the plank in my own eye I need to deal with before I start to worry about the speck in yours.

Shadows

*People brought the sick into the streets . . . so
that at least Peter's shadow might fall on some
of them as he passed by.* (Acts 5:15)

A person's shadow has, in some cultures, significance and power. It is said that people from villages in India would maneuver themselves to a place where Mahatma Gandhi's shadow might fall on them and thereby bring them blessing. At the same time they carefully avoided any possibility that their own shadows might touch—and so depreciate—his noble presence.

We do not share the superstition that a shadow literally represents the good or ill that a person brings into the world, but it is worth considering that each of us does cast a shadow of some kind. We do have an influence. Some are better for having drawn close to us; some may be worse. Love and caring seem to encourage more love and caring, while neglect and abuse seem to foster more of the same. The shadows that fall upon us influence the shadows we cast upon others, and like ripples in a pond they continue unstopped until they reach the far shore.

Jack Alwin, my sophomore English teacher in high school, taught me to love poetry. I taught it briefly to high school students myself and heard from two of them later that they were preparing to become English teachers so they could share with others the love for poetry they had learned from me. It caused me to wonder whose shadow had first fallen on Mr. Alwin.

The story is told of an American medical student who studied in Europe many years ago. He finished his courses and decided, rather than returning home to go into practice, to remain in Europe to encourage a friend who was having difficulty in his own studies. With help, that friend finally completed his degree and went to Africa as a medical missionary.

Years later the missionary wrote back to friends in France calling for more help in the work. His letter was read from pulpits throughout the land, and one who heard his plea was the minister's son in Alsace who himself determined to go to Africa as a doctor. His name was Albert Schweitzer. I wonder whose shadow had touched the life of that medical student two generations before.

"I have a little shadow that goes in and out with me," Robert Louis Stevenson wrote in his poetry for children. I cannot know all those upon whom my shadow may fall, but whoever they are, may they find it a healing influence of encouragement and love.

Weary

Come to me, all you who are weary and
burdened, and I will give you rest. (Matthew
11:28)

The waiting room at the Outpatient Clinic of the Heart Institute has ordinary waiting room dÈcor—large nondescript pale framed prints on the walls, gray industrial carpeting, low-backed arm chairs lined up like pews. Newspaper sections lie here and there, community property by midmorning. Earnest conversations too soft to be overheard become white noise, punctuated occasionally by the tune of a cell phone ringing. It is a weekday morning in a place where people get news about their futures, a room full of worries and fears.

A small, frail woman with a red hat pulled low on her head sips water from a foam cup, her pinched features, stooped shoulders and sad eyes betraying a hard life. Next to her in a wheelchair is a beefy man with a large shock of unruly gray hair. He is too big for his wheelchair, and his knees jut uncomfortably upward revealing sallow skin above black socks and shiny white athletic shoes. He stares fiercely at the red hat, his voice rising to become audible: "Did you not hear me? Don't you understand what I say?" She takes another sip, looking away, not wanting to be embarrassed, trying to deflect attention. She is thinking how nice it would be to visit her sister in Buffalo for a few days. But she will not go. What would happen to him if she left?

She is relieved when a moment later a nurse steps into the doorway. "Don?" the nurse asks, as though the name is unfamiliar to her. He scowls, drooping gray mustache accentuating his unhappiness. The red hat struggles to her feet, adjusting purse straps on her shoulder. It is all she can do to push the wheelchair of this difficult lump of a man, straining forward to keep this burden that is her life moving toward its destiny.

Then the wheelchair and red hat are back in the waiting room, rolling toward the elevator door. They stop at the water fountain where she refills her cup and offers him a sip. "Thank you," he says, touching her arm, the hint of a smile on his face. Apparently there is some good news from the doctor. Good news for the red hat too. A sign of kindness—a simple word of appreciation—has made the load a little lighter.

Heaven provides, I think, special mercies to those from whom love requires much but to whom it offers little. May they be blessed who persevere daily under a burden of unrelieved responsibility. Take heart in the promise of him who offers rest to the weary.

Whistling

But the Lord was not in the wind . . . , the
earthquake . . . (or) the fire. And after the fire
came a gentle whisper. (1 Kings 19:11, 12)

George was in his twenties when I knew his family many years ago. He was blind as well as mentally handicapped. His parents, Emil and Martha, a simple, elderly couple on the fringe of our church's life, did their best to care for him in every way. It was a difficult task, and they did it with great tenderness. Only Martha attended church—and rarely so—so I never saw Emil or George except on those occasions when I would visit in their home.

One day I stopped in and found Martha ironing. Embarrassed by the stacks of laundry standing around, she sent me out to the back yard to talk to her husband. He was working in their large and impressive garden, while George sat on the back porch, rocking. I greeted George and started down the steps toward Emil in the garden when I noticed the music. Emil was whistling as he worked, not any tune that I recognized but just notes—low and quiet and pleasant.

Later, over coffee, I mentioned it, saying that he must enjoy his gardening, since he whistled all the time. In his gruff, abrupt

129

way Emil said, "No, the whistling is for the boy. It lets him know I'm nearby."

People tell me occasionally that God has spoken to them and revealed one thing or another. I am not sure what they mean, unless it can be that they have found some resolution or confirmation of their desires and identify that to be God speaking. When I was a young man, a friend and mentor confronted me thoughtfully for the first time about the possibility of a career in ministry. I thought I heard the voice of God in his words because of their impact, but it is the only time I can say I have considered that God has "spoken" to me. As with Elijah, so also for me there has been no wind, no earthquake, no fire.

But God whistling—that I have heard. Every day brings reminders that God is around. The warmth of a friend, an answer to a problem, determination to get on with the job, courage to face a disappointment, redemption from a failure, the chance to help out—on and on the music goes, quiet, comforting and reassuring.

Listen for the whistling. It lets you know God is nearby.